OSPREY
PUBLISHING

Gladiators
100 BC – AD 200

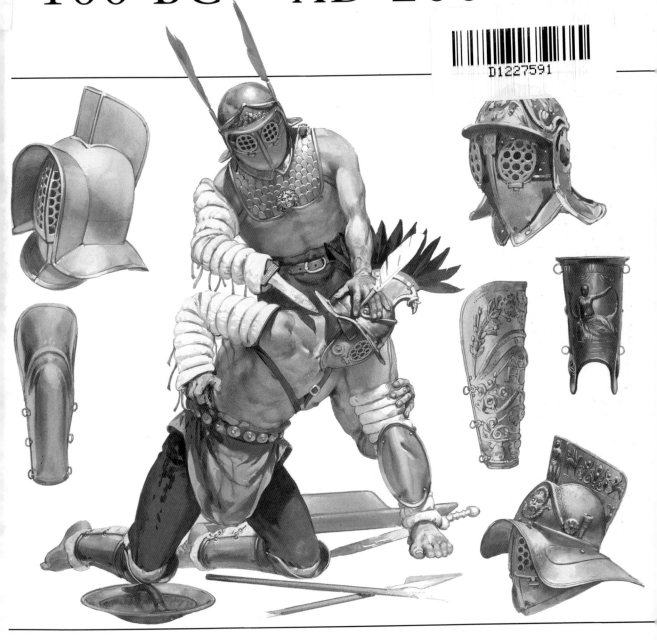

Stephen Wisdom • Illustrated by Angus McBride

First published in Great Britain in 2001 by Osprey Publishing, Elms Court, Chapel Way, Botley, Oxford OX2 9LP, United Kingdom.
Email: info@ospreypublishing.com

ISBN 1 84176 299 7

Editor: Nikolai Bogdanovic
Design: Ken Vail Graphic Design, Cambridge, UK
Index by Alan Rutter
Originated by Magnet Harlequin, Uxbridge, UK
Printed in China through World Print Ltd.

01 02 03 04 05 10 9 8 7 6 5 4 3 2 1

FOR A CATALOGUE OF ALL BOOKS PUBLISHED BY OSPREY MILITARY AND AVIATION PLEASE CONTACT:

The Marketing Manager, Osprey Direct UK,
PO Box 140, Wellingborough, Northants,
NN8 2FA, United Kingdom.
Email: info@ospreydirect.co.uk

The Marketing Manager, Osprey Direct USA,
c/o MBI Publishing, PO Box 1,
729 Prospect Avenue, Osceola, WI 54020, USA.
Email: info@ospreydirectusa.com

www.ospreypublishing.com

Artist's note

Readers may care to note that the original paintings from which the colour plates in this book were prepared are available for private sale. All reproduction copyright whatsoever is retained by the Publishers. All enquiries should be addressed to:

Scorpio Gallery, PO Box 475, Hailsham, East Sussex, BN27 2SL, UK.

The Publishers regret that they can enter into no correspondence upon this matter.

Author's note

My thanks to Jane, Griff, Rosie and Ridley. This book is dedicated to Les, Phil and Maureen for enduring the babble of a boy that breathed history and letting him make armour in the living room.

CONTENTS

GLADIATORS
100 BC – AD 200

INTRODUCTION

Scrawled on a wall in the ruins of the Roman city of Pompeii are the words, 'Celadus the Thracian – the girls' hero and heart-throb'. These few words reach out across the centuries, mute witness to a fascination that still captures our imagination just as it did when the city was buried by volcanic ash in AD 79. Whether seen through a lens of 21st-century Hollywood, or from a seat in the afternoon sun of an ampitheatre 2,000 years ago, images of Celadus and his fellow gladiators remain strong. Their world was not one of regimented legions or armed barbarian hordes, but of combat fought purely for entertainment, of slaughter for profit.

In the most famous of all Roman amphitheatres, the Colosseum in Rome, stands a crucifix. It was erected as a tribute to the Christian martyrs who were thought to have perished there in a variety of hideous ways, on the orders of successive pagan emperors. Nero, for example, executed Christians by *crematio*, burning them in pitch cloth. As these poor unfortunates suffered, probably in the location of the Vatican Hippodrome in Rome, they illuminated a further display of cruelty on the darkened floor below. Amphitheatres were purpose-built as locations for spectacles of death, displays that seem particularly cruel and barbaric today. Historians have praised the Romans for the 'civilising influence' of their empire, for the roads, aqueducts and heated baths that the settlers introduced. But this is to judge Roman values with our perception of what is regarded as civilised. The Roman concept of civilisation and culture included some very dark and, to our

The *scissor* gladiator in a relief carving from the east of the empire. It is believed this fighter used the traditional blade together with the unusual crescent-shaped blade to parry the blows of the *retiarius*. (Author's illustration)

modern eyes, barbaric practices. The gladiatorial games of the Colosseum and other amphitheatres of the Empire rank as particularly unpleasant.

Roman peoples viewed barbarism in a different way. To them, the remaining unconquered tribes of Europe were inferior because they had no understanding of the Roman world and style of living; they were therefore regarded as barbaric, rude and uncultured. Roman rule was more than a method of government. It was a way of life, which offered material and technological benefits to those who embraced it. Tribal kings were encouraged to adopt Roman culture in their style of rule. They became puppet kingdoms, at the bidding of the imperial master. But this stability and material gain had a price attached to it. The bloody displays of death and punishment in the amphitheatres were openly marketed as public entertainment but also subtly served to emphasise, by the deaths of criminals, captured rebels or prisoners of war, that Rome would not tolerate those who destabilised the dominion it had worked so hard to develop. Rome's rules of law had to be seen to punish law-breakers.

Throughout history, death and execution have been punishments for what the executioners perceive as criminal acts. Criminals, in a civilised society, are unwanted members of society. Extremist regimes have extended this argument so that anyone who is unwanted is regarded as a criminal, and is therefore expendable. In the Roman Empire, just as in successive centuries, the guilty (in Roman eyes) were executed. Those who suffered for their religious convictions at the Colosseum did so because they were seen as enemies of the community who disturbed the harmony that the imperial regime liked to project as part of the benefits of its rule. Those who died were often guilty by association, but there were other victims as well, such as arsonists and temple robbers. Murderers committing parricide could also expect death in the arena. Seneca recorded that the public execution of criminals was not merely entertainment: '[The purpose of executing criminals in public] is that they serve as a warning to all, and because in life they did not wish to be useful citizens, certainly the state benefits by their death.'

In their grandest form, gladiatorial combats could use thousands of captured criminals, prisoners of war or slaves in the vast recreation of a

Talamonius, **as depicted on the Galleria Borghese mosaic. He wears what seems to be the accepted look of a late 4th- century** *retiarius,* **with a scale or mail arm guard and the practical strapping across his chest preventing it from moving. (Author's illustration)**

Roman military victory. Such displays reinforced the superiority of Rome over the barbarian enemy, and provided an entertaining and spectacular day out for the Roman mob, where one might actually see a man, or men, be killed. The Romans believed that gladiatorial spectacles allowed the condemned combatants to display a quality rooted in Roman moral values, that of *virtus*, or vitue. They had the chance to show bravery and spirit as they were attacked; in death they could elevate their barbarian lives to a higher level. They may not have embraced Roman culture, but they could at least die like Romans should.

Single fighters were the highlight of any games day, but were a breed apart from the desperate criminals who killed each other in mass battles. These 'armoured fighting men', the *hoplomachi*, were what we now associate with the term 'gladiator'. They fought with the *gladius* or short sword, but shared a common purpose with their criminal fellow fighters. Whether locked in single combat or in epic battle on a grand scale, these combatants were encouraged to draw their opponent's blood and prolong his suffering, simply to entertain the public with the sight of blood spilling on to sand.

Not all gladiators were dispossessed or criminals. Drawn by the lure of big winnings – or merely for the thrill of it – some volunteered for the profession and a few became so popular with the citizens of the towns and cities of the empire that their fame spread from tavern to imperial palace. Their names appeared on walls in towns, and polite society, the chattering classes of ancient times, spoke about them at dinner parties. For a period of nearly 600 years, the arena was one of the most popular entertainments in the Roman world, and few found it unpleasant, or doubted its validity as a good example of the power of the Roman way of life. From citizen to Caesar, the gladiators gave the Roman audience blood, and the audience loved them for it.

Pampines, as depicted on the Galleria Borghese mosaic. Unusually he seems to be wearing a full length breastplate, together with *myrmillo* or *provocator* equipment. (Author's illustration)

BELUREFONS

CUPIDO

'Cupido dies at the hands of the *secutor* Belurefons.' Cupido's name is followed by the death symbol showing that this was to be his last appearance in the arena. His killer is wearing the crested helmet of a *secutor*. (Author's illustration)

CHRONOLOGY

509 BC	Rome becomes a republic.
264 BC	Sons of the late Brutus Pera stage three pairs of gladiators who fight to the death in a location called the Forum Boarium in Rome.
216 BC	As many as 22 gladiators are ordered to fight in the Forum Boarium, at one occasion. Like Brutus Peras' funeral games, the displays are in public, turning previously private funeral arrangements into a public entertainment to glorify the dead.
174 BC	Flaminius's games in Rome feature 74 fighters, an unprecedented number, who fight over three days. Fights now are staged in the Forum Romanum, where a wooden amphitheatre has been built.
165 BC	The playwright Terence complains that his popular play *The Mother in Law* is abandoned by the audience, because someone announces a gladiatorial contest is starting in the arena nearby.
73 BC	The gladiator Spartacus rebels with 70 fighters from the school at Capua.
65 BC	Julius Caesar attempts to stage a show of gladiators for his dead father, but political rivals feel jealous of Caesar's efforts and pass a bill limiting the numbers of fighters an owner can hold. 640 gladiators still fight to the death during the period of the games.
46 BC	Julius Caesar stages infantry, cavalry and elephant battles totalling more than 1,200 fighters.
29 BC	Amphitheatre of Titus Statilius Taurus built of wood and stone in Rome.
AD 37–41	The emperor Caligula feeds criminals to wild animals in the wooden arena in Rome to entertain the mob.
AD 44	The emperor Claudius recreates the sack of a British town, using elaborate props and set constructions in Rome's amphitheatre of Titus Statilius Taurus.

AD 64	During Nero's reign, the great fire of Rome destroys the city's largest wooden amphitheatres.
AD 70	The Flavian Amphitheatre, the Colosseum, is begun in Rome, on the redundant site of the late Emperor Nero's Golden House palace. The site features an ornamental lake, cleverly designed into the new arena floor for naval combats. There are no underground passages beneath the arena floor at this time.
AD 79	Pompeii and Herculaneum are destroyed in the volcanic eruption of Mount Vesuvius. The amphitheatre and gladiatorial barracks are preserved almost fully intact and the 63 bodies of trapped gladiators and visitors are buried beneath the ash with their arms and armour.
AD 80	The emperor Titus opens the Colosseum in Rome, capable of seating 50,000 people. Casualties among gladiators during the opening ceremony are unprecedented in gladiatorial combat. Along with chariot racing, the arena is now the most popular mass entertainment in the Roman world.
AD 107	The emperor Trajan stages a four-month period of entertainment with 10,000 fighters in the Colosseum. Thousands of fighters perish.
AD 180	Commodus becomes emperor and takes to the arena in the armour and weaponry of a *secutor*. He is a regular visitor to the imperial gladiatorial schools where he has elaborate rooms.
AD 192	The emperor Commodus is murdered and his gladiatorial armour is sold off. He has fought 735 times, but Victor, an ancient chronicler writing later, alleges that opponents were given lead weapons.
AD 380	Christianity becomes the official Roman religion. The Church rules that gladiators, their trainers and anyone concerned with the games are ineligible for baptism. To a lesser degree gladiatorial combat persists.
AD 399	Gladiatorial schools close for want of pupils as gladiators have become less interesting to the public. Condemned men are sent to the mines rather than to the schools, drying up a source of recruits. The public ceremony of Christmas becomes the accepted way to celebrate the winter solstice.
AD 404	Telemachus the monk runs into the arena and appeals to the assembled arena crowd to stop the fights. He is stoned to death by 'die hard' gladiatorial enthusiasts.
AD 404	The emperor Honorius uses Telemachus' example as a reason to finally close the arenas. Gladiatorial combat rarely takes place as its popularity is very much in decline. Historians believe it still persists as late as AD 439–40
AD 681	The Ostrogothic leader Theodoric apparently denounced a combat in AD 523 but gladiatorial combat is all but finished. It is finally officially banned in AD 681.

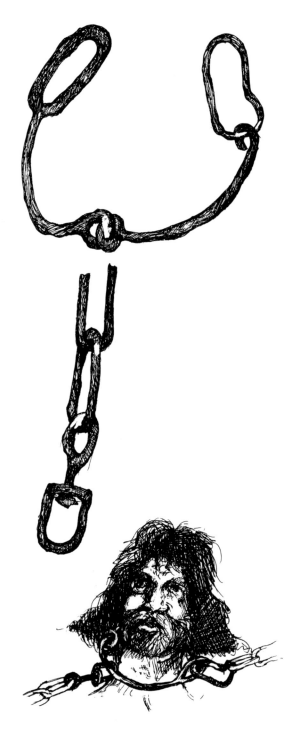

Slave chain from Colchester, Essex, England. This iron loop and chain are made to fit around the neck of a slave. The hinging loop on one end passes through the opposing loop and is held in place by the addition of another length of chain to another slave. Thus many prisoners can be held in a line. (Author's illustration, after item held at Colchester Castle Museum, Essex)

This relief shows two female fighters, Amazonia and Achilia. Note that they wear no helmets. Their helmets may possibly be displayed either side of their names: alternatively, they may be Podium fighters, the 'heads' therefore being their audience below. Careful study has enabled historians to recreate the hairstyles of each fighter (see page 45). (British Museum, London)

HISTORICAL BACKGROUND

For over 1,000 years Roman law governed thousands of square miles of Europe, North Africa and the Middle East. Influenced by both Greek and Etruscan culture, the Romans warred with the powerful Carthaginian Empire and after successive military victories developed a strong conquering army which gradually absorbed most of Europe as provinces of the Roman Empire.

Roman culture and civilisation were what separated the Roman people from the uncivilised barbarian tribes of unconquered Europe. Technological advances such as running water and heated floors were outward manifestations of a better way of life. Even the poorest citizen in Rome could expect regular distributions of grain. For the most part, Romans lived with a reasonable degree of security brought about by the efforts of Rome's generals and impressive military forces. They were justifiably proud of their martial heritage, which had provided them with so much.

The new provinces in which they lived had often been the site of battles in which the victory of Rome had been bought at the price of many legionaries' lives. To live in a *colonia*, a new town of settlers, was

ABOVE LEFT **Dwarf gladiator in bronze. Dwarfs were sought after as valuable fashion items in private houses where they served as attendants to men and women of high society. Here, one wears the equipment of a *hoplomachus*. (British Museum, London)**

ABOVE RIGHT **With his finger raised to appeal for mercy this bronze finial in the shape of a Thracian gladiator remains one of the most characteristic images of death in the arena. Note the extravagant plumes on the helmet. (British Museum, London)**

therefore a matter of pride to Romans. They were experiencing the fruits of their labours, the benefits of Romanisation, what they called the *Pax Romana*. To turn their backs on the culture that had given them the security of a new life in a strange country would have been unthinkable, not to say foolhardy. Settlers in newly formed Roman towns could immerse themselves in the culture of the empire itself. They were at liberty to embrace the government and religion that upheld the life they enjoyed.

The Roman Empire was influenced by Greek traditions as well as the earlier Etruscan style of fighting and war. Rome became a hybrid of different cultures, adopting, for example, both the gods of the Greek pantheon and Etruscan perceptions of death and the afterlife.

The belief that the gladiatorial fights evolved from Etruscan sacrificial death rituals is now widely believed to be false. However, we know that at the funeral of Brutus Pera, in 264 BC, the Greco-Syrian historian of the Augustinian age, Nicolaus of Damascus, notes that on Pera's instructions, his two sons paid for three simultaneous combats to take place in a cattle market. Within 100 years the custom of funereal contests between slaves owned by the organiser had become so accepted that in 174 BC Titus Flamininus held the *munus* (service to honour the dead) in Rome itself, matching 74 men against one another in a display lasting three days.

These *munera* tended to take place in December, coinciding with the festival of Saturnalia which honoured the god Saturn, the deity linked with human sacrifice. But the *munera* served a greater purpose than merely commemorating the dead. Animal hunts, or *venationes*, also took place. They were the morning spectacles, where hundreds of exotic animals from the far reaches of the empire were despatched by trained killers, the *venatores*, in a variety of bloody ways. The *venatio* symbolised the subjugation of vicious animals that Roman authority had encountered. These battles of lions, tigers and other highly dangerous creatures illustrated that Rome was victorious not only over men, but also the savage creatures of the world. Any culture that did not embrace Rome was therefore barbarian and worthless, fit only to be conquered by the vastly superior Romans.

The festival of the Saturnalia, taking place at the end of the year, meant that the audience had an opportunity to reflect not only on the dead man or woman honoured by the *munera*, but also on their own bereavements. As more noblemen, statesmen and provincial townsmen saw that *munera* were an effective monument to their lives, they began to make provision for them in their wills. It was no longer enough to stage a combat with several pairs of fighting men. The shows must be memorable, both in the number of casualties and style. Gradually, *munera* became more spectacular and expensive. Armour evolved to be more visually exciting, sometimes imitating the styles of the conquered peoples. *Munera* eventually became more than just a popular memorial to a dead official; they became a popular political statement, propaganda glorifying Rome.

With payments for musicians, officials and the support staff at an amphitheatre (armour was often captured from the enemy and was thus 'free'), men could not afford to impair their good name and memory by being mean with their money for their own *munus*. Many wills made provision for funerary games in honour of the deceased, and it seems that people expected a lavish *munus* when a notable person died. In Pollentia (Pollenzo, near Turin, Italy), Suetonius recorded that the townspeople forcibly prevented the funeral of one official, a former centurion, until his heirs had arranged funerary games that they could enjoy. This was no mere disruption of the town's peace. It appears to have become a full-blown riot, such was the strength of feeling, forcing Tiberius to send units of troops to quell the unease. One dying man stipulated that the combats at his funeral be between his ex-lovers. As they were all young boys, mercifully and with unusual sensitivity, the public annulled the will.

The bronze shield of a *hoplomachus*. Simply decorated, this concave disk would still afford reasonable protection against swordsmen in the arena. (British Museum, London)

The entertaining spectacle of the *munera* culminated in the gladiatorial games, often performed in purpose-built arenas. The first were constructed in amphitheatres in the capital around the Forum Romanum. They were made of wood and the arena floor was covered with *harena*, or sand, the origin of the word 'arena'. Some dreadful accidents took place in the overcrowded structures and Tacitus recorded what must rank as one of the worst. He says it was as destructive as 'a major war, it began and ended in a moment. An ex-slave called Atilius started building an amphitheatre at Fidenae for a gladiatorial show, but he neither rested its foundations on solid ground nor fastened the wooden superstructure securely … Lovers of such displays flocked in. Their numbers swollen by the town's proximity … The packed superstructure collapsed.'

Ironically, relatives of those who had gone to see the suffering of others, now quarrelled and fought over the bodies of their loved ones who, having been a long time beneath the ruins whilst recovery was on its way, were now unrecognisable. Tacitus says that 50,000 people died, though this may be an exaggeration.

With the building of the Flavian Amphitheatre, later known as the Colosseum, Rome had a remarkable new stone amphitheatre. The floor was originally of sand, but in later years it was rebuilt to provide a network of tunnels, the *hypogeum,* fitted with lifts and pulleys to assist in scenery changes, or trap doors to the surface for the speedy arrival of animals and fighters.

Sculpture of a Thracian gladiator. Note the curved short sword identifying this style of fighter. (British Museum, London)

The architectural archaeologist Jean-Claude Golvin, in his definitive text *Amphitheatres et Gladiateurs,* has identified at least 186 amphitheatre sites throughout the Roman world. There may be another 86 possible sites as well, which gives a clear idea of just how popular the gladiatorial spectacles were. Romans undoubtedly enjoyed the sight of others suffering, a predilection which should be put in context of the more violent age in which they lived. The Roman ideal of manhood placed great value on strength and martial training. They viewed single combat as a huge achievement, be it in the arena or on the battlefield. Good examples of the Roman spirit provided role models for how to behave in combat. The writer Valerius Maximus mentions Aemilius Lepidus, who, though only 15 years old, fought bravely against a Greek Phalanx of men, and used the open nature of the Republican battle line in his favour. He 'advanced into battle, killed an enemy soldier and saved a fellow citizen'. What young Aemilius possesed, in the eyes of the Romans, was the all important *virtus* or virtue. He was *Primarium Bellatorem,* he excelled as a warrior, and his martial efforts elevated him from mere nonentity to a role model for a citizen of the republic or empire. He so impressed his fellow citizens that they had a coin minted showing his exploits and erected a statue in his honour.

Gladiators, considered by many, including Cicero, to be 'ruined men or barbarians' could face death bravely. It was this bravery that was meant to inspire the watching audience. In the mind of a Roman citizen, proud of his culture and domination of the enemy, the gladiator of the arena was a good example to fellow citizens. If fighters who were *perditi homines,* the lowest of the low, could show bravery in the arena, or if one so *infamis* (untrustworthy*)* could actually show some bravery and mettle, just think what a *real* Roman citizen could achieve.

RECRUITMENT

Few Roman citizens would choose to become a gladiator. To call someone a gladiator was an accepted term of abuse. Seneca notes that one method of consoling a mother who had suffered the premature loss of a son, was to suggest that 'had he grown older he might have squandered his fortune and sunk to the level of fighting as a gladiator'. The hypocrisy of social attitudes towards gladiators caused some, among them the Christian writers Tertullian and St Jerome, to openly attack the senators and professional citizens who regarded gladiators as the social equivalent of prostitutes, but also followed their actions in the arena with great interest. It is this paradox, their poor ranking in society against their seemingly exciting life and chance of wealth, which drew men of sometimes good rank to the profession. Gladiatorial schools acquired most of their fighters from slave markets, but there were also a few volunteers among the ranks of new intakes of trainees.

Bronze Thracian fighter. The finely cast feathers either side of his helmet crest are still visible. Several helmets still bear plume mounts. (British Museum, London)

Some of these men would be broken individuals who had spent their inheritance, while others were there simply for the thrill. Of the rest, a high percentage were bought at the market, perhaps slaves, fallen from grace and sold by their masters. Historian Michael Grant estimates that for every ten men accepted into the gladiatorial schools, at least two were free.

The *ludi gladiatori,* the gladiatorial schools, imposed a harsh regime of discipline upon their trainee fighters. To promote *virtus,* the school operated a punishing schedule of physical exercise and practice, but also employed skilled *unctores* (masseurs) and *doctores* (fight trainers) to keep promising fighters healthy and fit. For the gladiator's colleague, the *venatores,* who wrestled and slew animals in the arena, there were similar services available.

It was in the schools' interests to keep their inmates relatively healthy. The shadow of the gladiator revolt of 73 BC not only shaped the public perception of gladiators as violent troublemakers, but also reminded the schools of the consequences of too harsh a regime of discipline.

Bronze *retiarius* gladiator. Though the fragile trident is now missing, this small *retiarius* figurine illustrates the size and defensive protection that a *galerus* armguard would provide. (British Museum, London)

The revolt of Spartacus, 73–71 BC

In 73 BC the gladiator Spartacus, enraged by the harsh treatment of gladiators, led a rebellion of gladiators against their masters in Capua, in southern Italy. The Greek writers Plutarch and Appian recorded that Spartacus and a fellow gladiator, a Celt called Krixus, overpowered the guards using kitchen knives. Spartacus' troops rode through the rural population inspiring slaves from the middle part of Italy to overthrow their masters. The rebels built a camp on the slopes of Mount Vesuvius, but the only road to the summit was guarded by the regular army forces of Claudius Glaber. Plutarch says that Spartacus fashioned a series of rope ladders of knotted vine branches that allowed them to descend the other side of the mountain. With arms and men they struck the unprepared Glaber in the rear and destroyed his force. As Spartacus' troops increased in number, the divisions between him and Krixus became deeper. The two rebels finally parted company, taking their respective forces with them. Krixus' troops were beaten near Mount Garganus by four legions under Lucius Gellius and Lentulus Clodianus, but Spartacus destroyed the Roman forces and, in a mockery of the trade he himself had been pressed into, forced his Roman enemies to fight to the death in gladiatorial combats, to appease the spirit of the fallen Krixus.

After a series of setbacks and marches Spartacus' troops found themselves facing the forces of Crassus, one of the most powerful leaders in Rome, who had gained his military experience with the great Roman general Sulla. Crassus' troops finally overcame Spartacus and he was slain. His followers could choose between a return to slavery or terrible crucifixion, the punishment for 6,000 of his followers along the Via Appia between Rome and Capua.

'We who are about to die' – the condemned criminals

Neither gladiator nor *venatores* suffered treatment as dreadful as the condemned *noxii*, the criminal elements of society who had been found guilty of robbery, rape or murder. Having lost their rights, they were now certain only that their prison life would end in the arena. For the *noxii* there would be no massage or schooling in the arts of fighting. They would be disposed of publicly, simply by thrashing and hacking their way through fellow *noxii* in the arena. Historians believe they may well have also been armed but un-armoured, fighting in exhibition killings against fully armoured veteran gladiators, whose sole purpose was to spill their blood. It is vital to keep these differences between the trained and the untrained in mind when attempting to understand the life of a potential volunteer or pressed man in the barracks and in the arena.

Acquisition of fighters

The slave markets were the best place to buy prospective members of any *familia gladiatoria*, a group of gladiators owned by their trainer/manager the *lanista*. *Lanistae*, usually themselves successful, freed ex-gladiators, recognised the qualities of a good fighter, but were regarded by society as the lowest, for they profited from the deaths of others with no physical risk to themselves. He was the same as a pimp or a procurer of prostitutes. In an effort to elevate himself to polite society one describes himself as '*Negotiator Familiae Gladiatoriae*', a 'business manager of a gladiatorial troupe'.

The *lanista* knew that his audience would appreciate both physique and good looks. At Pompeii, Crescens the *retiarius* gladiator (who fought with a net) was 'the netter of girls in the night', according to crude graffiti. Successful gladiators were sought as lovers by both men and women across the social strata. The body of a richly dressed woman was found with several male bodies at the barracks at Pompeii. It was even whispered that Faustina, the wife of the emperor Marcus Aurelius, had xxx indulged in affairs with gladiators, although this rumour was spread to explain her son's (the future emperor Commodus) passion for the sport as a teenager.

Under the emperors, prices for potential gladiators began to be strictly controlled. An inscription from Seville sets the accepted maximum prices for the categories of gladiators throughout the empire.

Danaos – a new recruit

Using original sources as a base, the author has reconstructed the life and career of a 2nd-century gladiator named Danaos, whose tombstone is preserved in the Kunsthistorisches Museum in Vienna, Austria.

Whether Danaos was a pressed man or a volunteer, he would have been selected by the *lanista* for his muscle and height. The average size of the Roman dead at Herculaneum, according to archaeologist Sara C. Bissel, who made a study of the skeletons, was 1.65m (5ft 4in) for men and 1.55 m (5ft) for women. The Roman cavalryman recently found by the waterside excavations was 1.73m (5ft 6 ¾ in) tall and this reflects the preferred size for combat soldiers and gladiators.

Danaos and his fellow gladiators would have been taken to the barracks by cart or on foot. Gladiators were not trusted by society, not

This small bone fragment is inscribed with the date and month in which a gladiator named Moderatus was released from the service of one Lucceius. (British Museum, London)

simply because of their low social position, but because, since the days of Spartacus, they had a reputation for rebellion and mutiny. Soldiers and security guards would watch Danaos at all times, vigilant for suicide and break-out attempts. It is likely that he and the prisoners of war also bought at the slave markets would be wearing slave chains, which severely incapacitated the wearer.

After unloading in the secure courtyard of the school, it would be clear that other members of the new *familia* were not pressed but had volunteered. These were the freemen and they were not chained, presumably because they posed no threat to security. Freed slaves were highly sought-after, and their treatment considerably better; *lanistae* believed they were more keen than their pressed fellows and would make a better show. Petronius Arbiter, in his novel *The Satyricon*, has his character Trimalchio extol the virtues of a visiting gladiatorial troupe saying 'a three-day show that's the best ever – and not just a hack troupe of gladiators but freedmen for the most part!'

Examples of gladiatorial art can be found on many household goods from the empire. On this oil lamp, typical of those sold outside any number of amphitheatres on the day of the games, a fallen fighter is despatched from behind by the victor. (Author's illustration)

Occasionally the offspring of the elevated classes of society entered the arena, Petronius Arbiter mentions a woman of the senatorial class fighting as a female gladiator. One account from Lucian of Samosata, who detested the arena, details the actions of Sisinnes, a man who enrolled at Amastris on the Black Sea in order to win 10,000 drachmae to ransom his friend out of captivity. Society's low regard for gladiators meant that such enlistment brought terrible shame on them. They had become the *infamis* – deprived of personal dignity and outside respectable society. Like prostitutes, Danaos and the others had sold their bodies for money.

But for some men the lure of the arena and the challenge of combat made the desire to take part too strong – even for an emperor. The emperor Commodus (AD 180–192) had been obsessed with gladiatorial combats since he was a child, which prompted political enemies of his father Marcus Aurelius to speculate that he was the son, not of the emperor but of an unknown gladiator. He certainly spent much of his youth in the company of gladiators. As an adult, he fought in the bejewelled and gilded armour of a *secutor*. At the time of his assassination he was said to have won

ASTYANAX

KNE NAⲤ⟁O Φ

over 700 bouts in the arena, but Victor, a contemporary writer, claimed that his opponents were armed with lead weapons.

Whether the emperor Commodus was asked to swear the gladiatorial oath '*Uri, vinciri, uerberari, ferroque necari*' ('to endure burning with fire, shackling with chains, to be whipped with rods and killed with steel') is lost to us, but the gladiators standing with Danaos would have to repeat the phrase as part of their induction. The shackling of chains was clearly a reference to the bonds about their necks, and the whipping with rods described the sticks that the *lanistae* used to encourage gladiators into fighting each other. Killing with steel spoke for itself. Danaos and the others would be led away to their small lockable cells around the perimeter of the training field to reflect on the life ahead of them. For the volunteers, the decision to join could be reversed in an instant with a cash 'buy-out' fee to the *lanista*. For the pressed men, there would be only training in barracks and the arena to come. Whether prisoner of war or privileged Roman youth, all were now equal, the lowest rank of gladiators, the *tirones*, or trainees.

Enveloped in the net of the *retiarius* (Kalendio) the *secutor* Astinax endeavours to free himself. The next image in this mosaic sequence shows the *retiarius* defeated and the *secutor* advancing to kill the loser. (Author's illustration)

DAILY LIFE

Accommodation

The impressive gladiatorial barracks in Pompeii were not originally intended as living quarters. From AD 62 the building became a training centre for gladiatorial combatants who had been recruited in the area and were to fight in the equally impressive arena on the other side of the town. On the yellow walls of the plaster-rendered cells are the graffiti names 'Julianus', 'Augustianus' and Neronianus', which suggest the presence of imperially sponsored gladiators, but no clear records that

this was officially a training school have survived. Pompeii's damp cells tend to give the impression that all gladiators lived in shabby conditions, but in the hierarchy of the gladiatorial barracks, the newest fighters were housed in the poorest accommodation: the quality improved if they were victorious in the arena or if they were a freeman or volunteer. When they achieved the rank of *primus palus,* the highest grade of gladiatorial greatness, they could demand the best accommodation, and being a bankable commodity for their *lanista,* would probably get it.

Social life and daily routine

At the school in Pompeii the cell walls are covered with scratched graffiti which gives a valuable insight into the baser feelings of the men held there. Crudely scratched pictures of women, their names beneath, were commonplace, as was a small niche to house a statue of any god the gladiator chose to honour. The graffitti at Pompeii tell of the successes and failures of the cell's previous occupants. The inevitable lewd remarks about visiting prostitutes reminded the gladiator of the outside world beyond the perimeter wall. Volunteer gladiators were not expected to escape from their service and were not subject to such a vigilant regime of security as the pressed men. Even the pressed gladiators could have girlfriends, and children were not unknown. A child's body was found in the barracks at Pompeii, and in Smyrna (modern day Izmir, Turkey) the whole school of gladiators contributed to the funeral of the daughter of a fellow fighter. Throughout the Empire touching cases of liaisons between gladiators and those outside the walls of the barracks are recorded, but none are so heartfelt as the papyrus message below from an *amatrix,* or follower, who has lost her love.

> 'At the command of a proud man, *myrmillo*
> Among the net fighters, alas you are gone,
> Gripping in strong hands a sword, your sole weapon
> And me you have left in my anguish alone.'

This illustration shows what is probably the musical band that accompanied the *paegniarii* (see page 42), dressed as animals. The 'flute-playing bear' (*ursus tibicen*) and 'horn-blowing chicken' (*pullus cornicen*) demonstrate the burlesque nature of the warm-up. (Author's illustration)

The object of her desires, a *myrmillo* gladiator, had been selected by a sponsor of the games to fight against the trident-armed *retiarii*. When overpowered, he failed to impress the audience, who voted for his death. We do not, of course, know of the relationship that these two had, but regular marriages are recorded between gladiators and their lovers outside the walls of the school. One can only hope the writer of the scratched message found on a pot shard, and worn perhaps as a charm, had more luck in love. It reads simply 'Verecunda the Actress loves Lucius the Gladiator'.

Schools emerged throughout the provinces of the empire during the first and second centuries AD, staffed by *doctores* or fight trainers. Like the *lanistae*, the *doctores* were highly skilled ex-fighters, but each one would be a specialist in his own field of combat, knowing the best way to use weapons and armour. Physicians treated the inevitable grim injuries of the profession, and *unctores* (masseurs) toned the bodies of the gladiators. The *unctores* had a sideline in bottling the oily grease and skin scrapings to sell as a restorative to ageing ladies.

They shared their work with accountants, armourers, cooks and security guards. It was not unknown for trainee gladiators to take their own lives if they could not endure the harsh regime in the schools. *Lanistae* were keen to avoid such financial losses, as schools invested substantial sums of money into training their pupils. Gladiators who did not adhere to the strict discipline of the schools suffered equally strict and harsh punishment. The gladiatorial barracks at Pompeii houses a prison in which archaeologists recovered the skeletons of the jailed inmates. They also found leg irons for up to ten men who would have spent their harrowing punishment in this low-ceilinged room unable to stand up. Beatings and whippings by the *doctores* were also commonplace; this was the 'whipping with rods' referred to in the gladiatorial oath.

Given this stark regime, the fear of mutinous rebellion was never far away. To keep these potentially dangerous elements secure, the guards and soldiery at a gladiatorial barracks kept the inmates under lock and key. In 49 BC, however, Julius Caesar's vast gladiatorial troupe of 5,000 men stationed at Capua were billeted about the city, two to a household, to prevent any organised revolt by the fighters in an armed uprising.

Organisation of the schools throughout the empire

From the latter part of the 1st century Rome replaced the *lanistae* of the capital with another official. The provincial towns of the empire still

This relief from Smyrna in modern Turkey shows a *provocator* in a large bulbous helmet and *cardiophylax* breastplate. Note the *corona* wreaths he has won for victories of particular note. (Author's illustration)

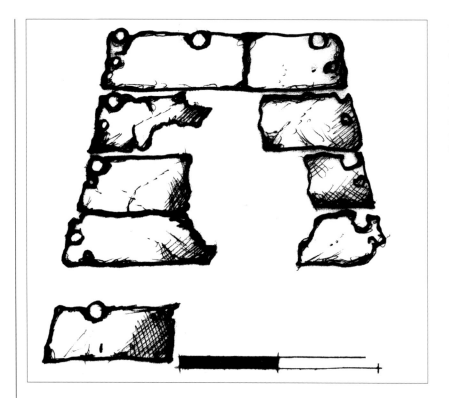

The Newstead excavations in Britain revealed bronze arm guards that were used in a legionary camp. Their use by gladiators is uncertain, but the Galleria Borghese mosaic shows what could be interpreted as metal bands on the arm. The measurement bar indicates 10cm (3.94in). (Author's illustration)

used *lanistae* to acquire fighters for clients, but from the reign of Domitian onwards (AD 51–96) games in Rome itself were organised directly by the imperial schools. The *lanistae* were replaced with *procuratores,* who were responsible both for the acquisition of fighters, and the general running of the four imperial schools, the *Ludus Magnus,* the *Gallicus,* the *Dacias* and the *Matutinus,* where *venatores* were trained. The *lanistae* in the rest of the empire assembled teams of gladiators at their own expense, often being subcontracted by wealthy clients, or *editors.* These were individuals who sponsored a games in order to increase their public profiles, usually for political reasons. After negotiating a price with the client on the understanding that perhaps half his stock could die, the *lanista* would purchase teams of fighters, although in some instances an *editor* hired them on an hourly basis.

Noblemen sometimes assembled teams of fighters themselves and employed freelance *lanistae* and *doctores* to train them. Cicero wrote to his rich friend Atticus, who owned a team of fighters, saying 'what a fine troupe you have bought. I hear your gladiators are fighting splendidly. If you had cared to let them out you would have cleared your expenses on the two shows you gave.'

If the lure of money drew desperate but brave fighters to the arena, then the comparatively risk-free profession of *lanista* appealed to shrewd businessmen. On a wall in Pompeii, Numerius Festus Ampliatus advertised his services as an itinerant *lanista.* He promoted himself by painting advertisements on stones (even gravestones) outside the town walls. According to Numerius himself, 'the whole world adores his troops of gladiators', but with no barracks or training ground his hack troupe of fighters might have found themselves performing in quickly adapted market squares and precincts.

TRAINING

Pliny the Elder was highly critical of the inmates of Caligula's school of gladiators, complaining that very few of them could refrain from blinking when a sword was shaken in their faces! Exacting training regimes were common all over the empire. Schools featured a series of buildings secured by a fence or wall around a training arena. The Ludus Magnus in Rome, the largest of the imperial schools (excluding its dining halls and store rooms), looked on first inspection like an amphitheatre. It featured the normal elliptical arena in which to train for and display fights, but the seating accommodation was much smaller. Here the *procuratores* would sit watching their valuable assets practising on the sand below them. As at Pompeii, the gladiators would dine in a refectory hall, eating specially prepared food said by physicians like Scribonius Largus to be healthy and muscle promoting. Gladiators were given the nickname of *hordearii*, or barley men, relating to the crop's benefits in protecting the arteries with fat that prevented heavy bleeding if cut.

Sharpened weapons were all but forbidden in the schools, the trainees at first being issued with wooden weapons for practice. A remarkable wooden sword was found at the legionary camp at Oberaden in Germany. Messy hacking and slashing bored the audiences, so the *doctores* were employed to teach the art of using the weapons to their best effect, both mortally and theatrically. As with the conventional Roman Army, novices would practise against a 1.7 metre-high (5 ½ ft) wooden post, the *palus*, at which they would thrash and strike to build upper body strength and stamina. A straw man, beloved of sword schools throughout history, could be substituted, giving a more accurate idea of an opponent's shape and vital areas.

Archaeologists have found heavy, oversized blunted iron weapons at the school in Pompeii. Opinion is divided as to whether these were for training or whether they were ornamental, belonging with the slightly larger than life-size martial statuary, which may have dominated the school's colonnaded grounds. Sharpened weapons (*arma decretoria*)

'Verecunda the actress (or prostitute) loves Lucius the Gladiator' is the translation of this pottery shard from the Jewry Wall Museum, Leicestershire, England. The hole indicates it was worn as a love charm.

CAMPANI VICTORIA VNI
CVMNVCERINIS PERISTIS

This graffiti from Pompeii shows a victorious fighter with his palm branch. 'Campanians,' it reads, 'you too were destroyed in our victory over the Nucerians'. This refers to a dispute between rival gangs of gladiatorial supporters within the walls of the city who used the riots of AD 59 to settle differences not only with the Nucerians of another district, but also each other. (Author's illustration)

were only issued in the arena, but Dr Marcus Junkelmann, an expert on Roman gladiatorial combat, suggests that volunteers and freemen were at liberty to use them if they so wished, being trusted thoroughly. With weapons, sharp or otherwise, gladiators would finally engage in practice fights, but if one became injured the fight would be stopped and the physician's work would begin. One wall painting shows the legendary hero Aeneas undergoing the removal of an arrowhead: such examples indicate that Roman medical practice, while primitive in some respects, was capable of treating serious flesh wounds with care (though the physicians were instructed to ignore the cries of the patient). A Roman medical kit of scalpels, hooks and forceps has recently been found in Colchester, England. Another is also displayed at the British Museum, London.

Fighters were armed in a variety of styles, each one equipped very differently and having a series of strong and weak points for their opposite number to attempt to take advantage of. Danaos was selected to fight as a Thracian. The resident physician treated any injuries he received in training. Galen of Pergamum, later to become the personal physician of the emperor Marcus Aurelius, considered, with unintentional irony, that his expert attention to the diet and health of gladiators in the barracks 'saved' many of their lives. As many later died in the arena, they were not spared for long.

APPEARANCE AND DRESS

The gladiatorial audience of the Roman world did not want to see the quick, economical death of soldiers. In the arena, 'theatre' rather than tactical military thought ruled supreme, and gladiators were equipped to look visually interesting rather than to be efficient and speedy in their disposal of an opponent. Their armour was originally simply the protection that prisoners of war had been captured with. In AD 44, the emperor Claudius recreated the capture of a British town, celebrating the triumph of his invasion of Britannia a year before. His 'tribal enemies', killed for the public delight, could have been prisoners captured in Britannia, wearing the armour of their fellow tribesmen. This accuracy of equipment lent a more theatrical feel to the event, but it was not a recent development. The earliest depictions of gladiators show simply dressed fighters, armed in the Samnite style of 310 BC. The Samnites introduced a new style of elaborate armour to the Romans that was radically different from Roman equipment and became to Roman people a stereotype for what the 'enemy' looked like.

These images evolved and merged with styles created by editors of the games to add to the drama of the contests. By the 2nd century AD people could spend a day in the *maeniana* (the public stands of an arena) often free of charge as an incentive to vote for the holder or *editor* of the games, watching a world of stylised mythical monsters and hunters. In the arena the 'fisherman', the muscular near-naked *retiarius*, armed with net and trident, stalked the half-man half-fish prey, the *myrmillo*, or *myrmilon*, armed with sword and shield, wearing a helmet crest shaped like a dorsal fin. The audiences thrilled to the combats of the griffin-crested Thracian against the plain-helmeted *secutor* (or pursuer).

Undergarments

All fighters, whether male or female, lightly or heavily armed, seem to have adopted the triangular loin cloth (the *subligaculum*) secured by a stout broad leather belt, itself laced or hooked together through a series of punched holes in each end. The wearing of this garment in the arena should not be seen as anything unusual as the *subligaculum* was normal Roman underwear. It was an equilateral triangle in shape, and modern reconstructions indicate it must have been at least 1.5 m wide at the edge. With one edge held horizontally behind the wearer in the small of his back, the two ends were tied together at the front as one would tie the arms of a sweater about your waist. The loose triangular material was then pulled tightly forward between the legs and tucked up under the knot at the front. What was left hung down at the front, the unsightly knots and rolls being covered by the broad leather *balteus* or belt. The Colchester Vase, a 2nd-century vessel found in Colchester, England, shows two fighters, Valentinus the *retiarius* and Memnon the masked *secutor*. What seem to be bells or decorative weights or beads hang from the hem of the *subligaculum* of Valentinus. The *balteus* could be decorated with a variety of embroidered metal or woven threads, as well as with fine embossing and plates of bronze.

The Colchester Vase is perhaps one of the best known images of gladiatorial combat in Britain. It shows the *secutor* Memnon achieving a victory over the *retiarius* Valentinus. Note what seem to be bells hanging from the *secutor*'s loincloth. (Colchester Castle Museum, Colchester, England)

Ironically, given the widespread death in the arena, public sensibilities were protected from the sight of bare-chested women fighters. Some sources believe that the female fighter covered her breasts with a wrap-around 'bandage', a *strophium* or later the *fascia*, made of damp leather, rather like the garment worn by civilian Roman women beneath the *stola* or gown. The British Museum exhibits a marble relief of two female fighters, one referred to in the inscription by her stage name, Amazonia. Sadly, her large shield covers all but a part of her chest, but the waistcloth is clearly shown.

The gladiatorial armouries of the imperial school at Rome, and elsewhere in the empire, would have housed a wide variety of helmets, shields and arm defences which were issued to fighters both in training and on the day of combat. It is not clear whether gladiators were dressed in their barracks and then taken to the arena, or whether they were dressed there. We do know that the archaelogical evidence at the amphitheatre at Caerleon in Wales suggests there were wooden dressing rooms, what actors call 'green rooms', where they could wait before their 'scene'.

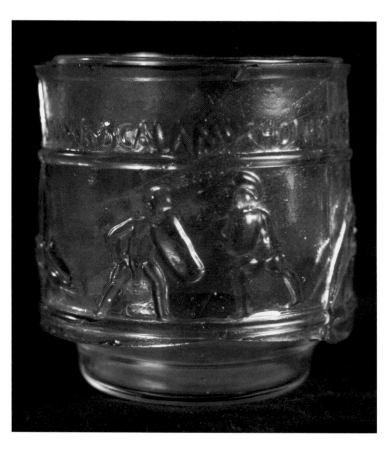

ABOVE **Early 1st-century glass beaker showing gladiatorial combat. This beaker is exceptionally rare and illustrates gladiators in different poses of combat. (Colchester Castle Museum, Colchester, England)**

ABOVE RIGHT **Reverse side.**

Fabric body protection

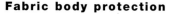

Gladiators probably did not wear shoes, although evidence in sculptures and mosaics occasionally suggests that a leather 'gaitor' was worn, perhaps to prevent the greaves on his legs chafing the upper part of the foot. Gladiators are rarely pictured wearing shoes, unlike their counterparts in the legions. A mosaic in the Romermuseum, Augst near Basel, shows *equites*-style gladiators who entered the arena on horseback, but fought on foot; they not only wear cloaks, but also dark shoe-like garments. Dr Marcus Junkelmann in his authoritative book *Das Spiel mit dem Tod*, has reconstructed several different styles of gladiator using his own interpretations of primary reference material. He has proposed that stout-soled overshoes, a continuation of the felt and quilted linen leg defences, were worn by some of the more heavily armed fighters.

Danaos, the Thracian gladiator, would have worn quilted fabric leg and arm defences. Tied on with leather thongs, the *fascia* on the legs and *manica* on the arms seem to have been common to all fighters from the 1st century AD. They are shown in many sculptures and mosaics, and their composition has been the subject of some debate. A bronze statuette of a *crupellarius* gladiator from Versigny, France, shows

heavy armour, and Tacitus asserts that they were 'entirely encased in steel'. The effectiveness of this kind of defence was shown in the Gallic revolt of Sacrovir in AD 21, when the legionaries were instructed to charge the rebels, who had recruited *crupellari* gladiators to their ranks. The legionaries had to break their way through the rebels using military pickaxes.

The Galleria Borghese in Rome houses one of the most important mosaics relating to the later period of gladiatorial combat in the 4th century. It is one of the clearest images we have today of the equipment of later-period gladiators. Gladiators are pictured wearing wrapped bandage material over their ankles. The historian Michael Grant, in his book *Gladiators*, quotes Juvenal the poet, who turns the full force of his ridicule on female fighters. He lists the equipment that this woman might have about her in the arena and includes, 'the rolls of bandage and tape, so her legs look like tree trunks'.

Modern day reconstructions suggest that lightly armed fighters would bind this tape over a felted padding, the thickness of this providing the 'tree trunk' of Juvenal's wit. A marble *stele* figure from Ephesus, Turkey (and similar Turkish finds from Izmir), show a very heavily armed gladiator (a *provocator*), whose padded garment extends beyond the upper left thigh, as well as fully down his right arm.

Metal leg and arm defence
The quilted protection offered by the *fasciae* was undoubtedly effective and the fighters who faced each other at the amphitheatres at Capua and Pompeii would have worn them. The 15 complete helmets found at Pompeii in the mid-18th-century excavation prove that metal defensive armour was not only practical, but was also fashioned to look striking and dramatic. From AD 100 the armour used in the western empire, the conquered area governed from Rome, changed very little, while the eastern empire, governed from Constantinople, continued to create new armour styles and combat schemes.

Despite the almost hysterical following of the fights in the arena, there were a few people in the amphitheatres who were actually interested in the skill of swordsmanship and for whom the armour worn would have a very important bearing on the outcome of the fight. They wanted to see blood spilling onto sand, but it was the way in which the respective fighters used their differing shield shapes and assorted

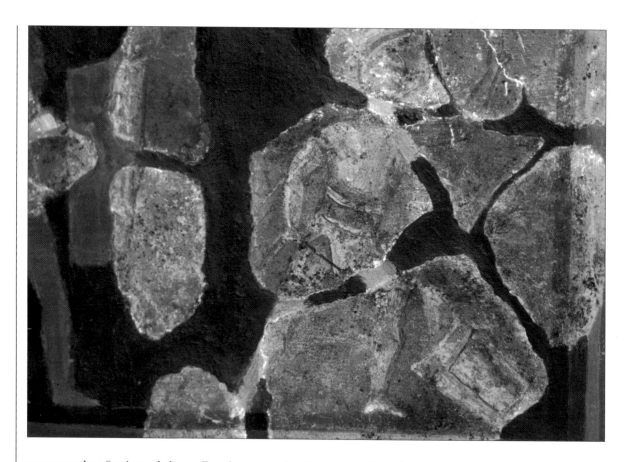

Fragmentary remains of a wall painting from Colchester, England, showing the surrender of a gladiator. At the time of this painting in the early 1st century, Colchester was the capital of Britannia and almost certainly had an amphitheatre and barracks.

weapons that fascinated them. For these people, Danaos equipped as a Thracian, for example, had to follow the established precepts of what a Thracian had always looked like, otherwise his skill at arms could not be fairly compared to another gladiator of his style. The same applies to every other type of gladiator. All had to follow a certain pattern of equipment, be they the double-daggered *dimachaeri*, the *scissores* with their bladed gauntlets, or the bizarre *andabatae*, about whom little is known. It is suggested that their helmets lacked eye holes, forcing them to thrash blindly at each other on horseback.

It was not unknown for gladiators wearing the requisite armour to have their allocation of equipment dramatically cut by the *editor* of the games, presumably to make the fight more interesting. The emperor Caligula reduced the defensive armour of the *myrmillo* fighters on a whim, as he preferred Thracian-style gladiators. History does not record whether anyone spoke out against this outrageous bending of the rules, but given the response of some emperors to criticism (the emperor Domitian is said to have publicly thrown a man to a pack of wild dogs for saying that a Thracian might beat the emperor's favourite *myrmillo*), it was hardly likely that anybody complained.

Assuming that the fights advertised for the day included the most common and successful forms of gladiator, then at least four different sets of armour would have been prepared by the slaves of the dressing room. Danaos, our Thracian fighter, would have two greaves or *ocreae* strapped to his lower leg bandaging. At Smyrna (Izmir), Turkey, a gladiator called Priscus is referred to in a relief as a Thracian and he wears the two greaves of his profession. This evidence is corroborated by other sculpture and painting throughout the empire. A pair of splendid greaves was discovered beneath the mud of Herculaneum near Vesuvius. Tied on to the leg through three sets of D-shaped rings riveted to the folded edge of the leg piece, they were each beaten from one piece of bronze. Greaves could be undecorated, but this pair have embossed pictures worked into them. The kneecap of each is decorated with a Gorgon's head, the shin being plain. The detail decoration of the left greave has a bearded head surrounded by a lozenge, and the right features pictures of Silenus, the mythological attendant of the god Bacchus, with the Maenads, his frenzied female companions, on the left. Another pair, identical in construction, show Jupiter bearing a lance surrounded by lightning.

The detail on greaves did not necessarily have to be embossed. Punched and engraved detailing is commonly found on armour of this period. An example of what might be punched and engraved work can be seen at Pompeii. The tomb of Caius Vestorius Priscus outside the Porta Vesuvio gate is decorated with large spectacular wall paintings, one of which shows two fighters, the plumed Thracian being the victor. His right leg is clearly covered with a large greave, on which the very faint traces of decoration are seen. He may also be wearing a padded and decorated garment on his upper leg as clear patterning is shown here also. Junkelmann suggests that a tight-fitting pair of trousers was optional.

Thracian gladiator (copy) based on an example from the 2nd century AD. The original was equipped with a curved sword that fitted into the right hand. (Author's photograph)

The Pompeii Thracian painting, dating from early in the empire, shows no metal *manica* (solid overlapping plates that can be seen in later images of this style of fighter). Historians speculated over the use of leather in the manufacture of *manicae*, but H. Russell Robinson, of the Royal Armouries, England, doubts it was widely used in armour construction.

By the time of the Dacian wars of the emperor Trajan in AD 106, gladiators must have been using some kind of segmented arm defence, as it is said to have influenced the development of a similar armour then issued to the legions in the field to protect them from the terrible injuries inflicted by Dacian slashing hooks. A great debate has circulated as to the likely construction of these metal *manicae*. The segmented iron fragments of a *manica* found at Newstead in Britain, were probably riveted to a series of leather strips running lengthways from the shoulder. Flexibility may have been a problem unless the *manica* incorporated an elbow plate, or Roman equivalent of the medieval *couter*. A relief of a *retiarius* gladiator, found at Chester (but currently in Saffron Walden Museum in Essex) clearly shows a *manica* defence with the crucial elbow couter, which appears to solve the problem, but is the only reference, as yet, discovered. The *manicae* were not only laced to the arm itself but also as the Galleria Borghese mosaic shows, they possessed a series of straps stretching across the chest, around the back and over the left shoulder where buckles united the ends.

The *manicae* may have been deliberately made in two separate ways, with the plates overlapping either from the shoulder down, or from the wrist up. Reconstructions in England by experimental armourers of the Second Legion Augusta re-enactment group have suggested that gladiators chose different styles of *manicae* depending upon the weapons of their opponents. The trident of the *retiarius* slashed upwards, for example, whereas a *myrmillo*'s weapon posed a horizontal threat. Later, in the 2nd and 3rd centuries AD, both mail and scale arm defences become familiar. It is generally believed that though military use of these materials was common, they were unused in gladiatorial circles until later.

Parade armour

Julius Caesar was reported to have issued top class gladiators with armour of solid silver, and Nero's men wore armour decorated with carved amber. Domitian attempted to dress his men in pure gold. As the top class gladiators entered the arena aboard chariots, they were dressed in purple cloaks fringed with gold, a fragment of such a cloak being found at Pompeii. The *pompa*, the parade at the start of a games, was organised on an extravagant scale by the *editor*. Peacock feathers were commonly used in plumes, with gold thread woven in tunics and *subligaculum*. The helmet in Naples so deeply embossed with a relief representing the 'Apotheosis of Rome' is probably a parade helmet for the opening

The gladiatorial barracks at Pompeii. The tiled colonnade has been partially restored to its 1st-century appearance. The grass enclosure between the four walls was the training field. (Author's photograph)

ceremony which would be replaced by a slightly simpler version for the fighting. When new it would have been polished bronze, but even the simpler combat versions would still have been impressively decorated. Only the *secutor*'s helmet was plain, so as to avoid snagging the net of the *retiarius*.

Helmets and headgear

Gladiatorial helmets were intended to protect the wearer and thus prolong the fight. The 'fun' for the audience would be taken out of the combat if a fighter received a stunning blow that rendered him insensible or, worse, unconscious. A prone man is not entertaining.

Padding inside helmets, either military or gladiatorial, has long been a point of discussion. It is likely that a thick-well-felted, fabric lining in four segments was cemented in place with glue and was thick enough to keep the helmet in place in combat. At Newstead, Britain, a fragment of thick coarse fabric has been found on the inside of a cavalry helmet, and the visor shows clear traces of a resinous substance which when warmed became sticky. Excavations at Hod Hill, England have also revealed a military cheek plate with fabric glued inside.

The tomb of Vestorius Priscus at Pompeii is well worth a visit to see this remarkable pair of fighters. Standing by the Porta Vesuvio gate, travellers could see that although he died at the age of 22, Priscus enjoyed the martial sports in the arena. His mother commissioned the decoration of the walls with these two *myrmillo* fighters. (Author's photograph)

Many gladiators wore a headband, as well as a small band of tasselled rope or leather tied around their knees or upper arms. Opinion is divided as to its use, but it is common wear of many of the gladiators shown in the Galleria Borghese mosaic. The numbers of tassels are not the same; perhaps they acted as a visual 'scorecard', each victory represented by a fresh tassel.

The Thracian

Thracian helmets were instantly recognisable from the representation of a griffin on the peak of the crest. There are at least two helmets (*galea*) of the Thracian, Thraex or Thrax style on display in the Naples Museum of Antiquities. Another example is to be seen in Castel Sant'Angelo in Rome. Usually the helmet shell is in one piece, beaten from a solid piece of bronze. At the point where the brim is joined, the metal of the shell has been flared out, and the separate brim has been hammered over it, fusing the two together. The brim's edge is rolled to provide strength, and the two face plates are hinged just in front of the ears. The eye holes are covered with a grille of bronze pierced with nine round holes. According to modern reconstructions, the wearer has a good degree of forward vision and ventilation, but in a large-scale fight between many men (the rare, but not unknown, *gregatim*) it would not give effective side vision. A flanged defence beneath the chin would offer some protection against a slashing blow against the throat.

The amphitheatre at Pompeii, seen from the highest row of seating. Even though 64m (70 yards) away from the centre of the arena the excellent acoustics ensured that the women, who would have been allocated this position, would have been able to hear quite clearly the cries of a wounded fighter, unless they followed orders and kept as silent as possible. (Author's photograph)

The most recognisable feature is the griffin sculpture fixed to the forward tip of the crest. The detailed Herculaneum *myrmillo* 'parade' helmet has small rings either side of the crest to hold elaborate *crista*, plumes of ostrich or other exotic feathers, held in place with leather thongs in wooden mounts. Both *myrmillo* and Thracian sculptures illustrate these features. Smaller single feathers were placed in tubes above each ear in a style similar to military helmets of the same period.

Dr Junkelmann's experiments with reproduction embossed armour, copied from the Pompeii discoveries, show it is perfectly capable of withstanding a strike without serious buckling. The helmets weigh between 3.3 and 6.8kg (7 ¼ –15lb) and the thickness averages 1.5mm. A legionary's helmet weighed about 2kg (4 ½lb). While a gladiatorial helmet may seem heavy in comparison, Junklemann's research suggests that most contests lasted between 10 and 15 minutes, whereas legionaries had to wear their helmets all day.

The *myrmillo*

The equipment of the *myrmillo* differed only slightly from that of the Thracian. There were the obvious variations in helmet design, namely that the *myrmillo* had a huge dorsal fin in place of the Thracian's more reserved crest. The *mormylos* (or sea fish) had become the inspiration for this type of gladiator.

The *myrmillo* helmets found in Herculaneum and Pompeii are all based on a common theme and are similar in construction to the Thracian helmet. However, a spectacular *myrmillo* helmet in Berlin is both unusual in design and remarkable in construction and finish.

The gladiatorial barracks at Pompeii looking to the training ground. On days of poor weather or blistering heat this style of architecture afforded the *lanista* and his staff a sheltered position to view their charges, while keeping the doors of the gladiators' cells in the buildings cool. (Author's photograph)

When new it must have been a spectacular sight, being polished bronze with thousands of silver and gold chequerboard patterns over its surface. In the arena, with the sun upon it, the appearance would resemble the shimmering scales of a fish. This armour also includes a plainly finished, unembossed greave with a similar chequering.

The entry corridor to the theatre complex at Pompeii has many scrawls of fascinating graffiti from the pre-eruption period. It is a tribute to the gladiatorial enthusiasts who drew them nearly two millennia ago that their fighters are still recognisable today. Between the scribbles of modern tourists, two gladiators are clearly seen, one armed and shielded as a *myrmillo*, but unusually carrying a trident as a principle weapon. His opponent carries a sword and smaller shield. These naïve, stalky figures illustrate the appeal of the gladiators and the features which made them so recognisable in the arena, even when seen from a distance.

The *retiarius*

The trident was normally unique to the *retiarius*. *Retiarii* were usually handsome young men; the average age of a gladiator was between 18 and 25, although one was still fighting as late as his 40s. With minimal combat equipment, they used the 1.6m (5 ¼ft) trident or harpoon, the *fascina*, and a small dagger, the *pugio*. *Retiarii* were also equipped with a 3m (9ft 9in) diameter net, the *rete*, with which they could ensnare opponents, trip them, or whip them. The weights were like modern fishing weights and if lashed with sufficient power, the net could blind a man. Around the perimeter of the net was a rope, both ends of which

Training, Pompeii, AD 78

B

The *retiarius*
(see plate commentary for full details)

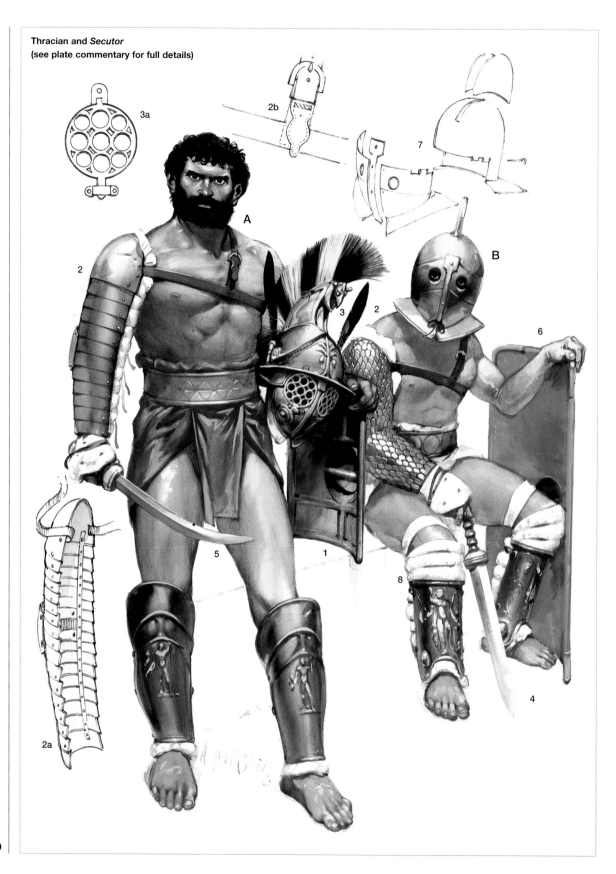

Thracian and *Secutor*
(see plate commentary for full details)

3a

2b

7

A

B

2

3

2

6

5

1

8

2a

4

D

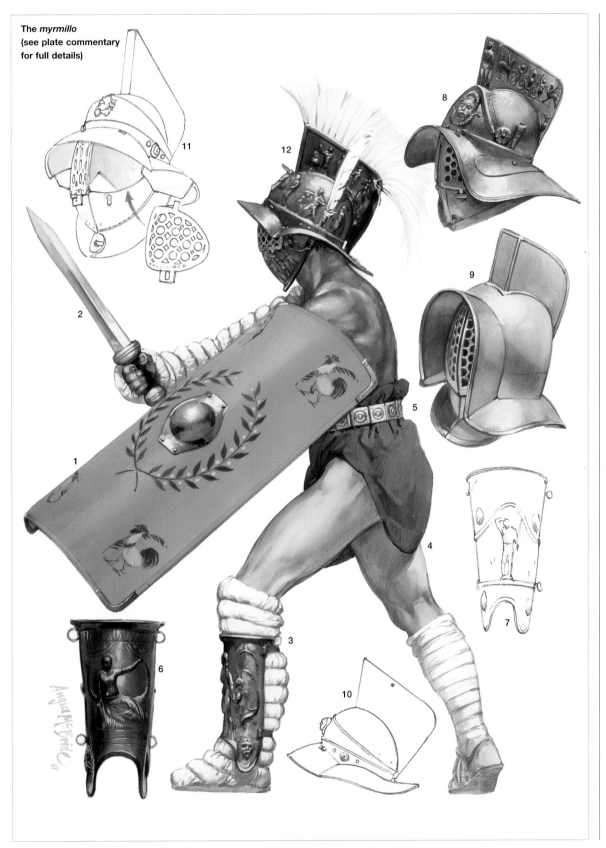

The *myrmillo*
(see plate commentary
for full details)

1

2

3

4

5

6

7

8

9

10

11

12

E

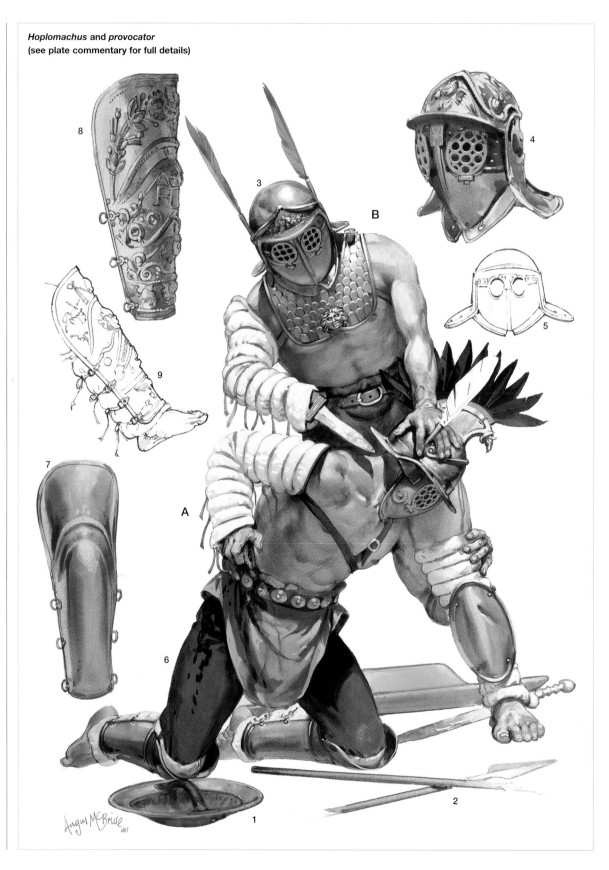

Hoplomachus and *provocator*
(see plate commentary for full details)

8

4

3

B

A

7

9

6

5

2

1

Angus McBride 001

F

The afternoon show: the *noxii*,
Pompeii, AD 78

GLADIATORES

ASTINAX

ASTINAX

A school of his own

H

The barracks refectory at Pompeii. Though now a crumbling shell, this large room once housed the dining room for the gladiators. It looked out on to the training fields. The rear door ran to the apartments and offices of the *lanista*. His private rooms, now sealed off, are decorated with numerous wall paintings of gladiatorial scenes. (Author's photograph)

severely restricted vision through eyeholes just 35mm (1¹⁄₃in) in diameter, the *secutor* fought in a visored helmet with a traditional infantry sword, the *gladius*. He wore perhaps one short greave on his left leg, the other being barefoot and uncovered. Reconstructions by Dr Junkelmann have illustrated that this helmet afforded great protection but severely limited sound and vision.

Other types of gladiator

The four styles of gladiators were the most common in the western empire, but it was not unusual to find specialised fighters on some programmes. Of these, a number of fighters must have posed a threat to the audience as well as their opponents. *Saggitarii* gladiators were armed with reflex bows capable of propelling an arrow a very great distance. They shot at each other across the arena, but the audience would undoubtedly have been in range of any stray arrows.

The *essedarii* fought from the *essedium*, the Celtic war chariot, in the style of the British. At least one of the *essedarii* was a woman, as is mentioned by the poet Martial. They also seem to have faced wild beasts. An engraved cup in Augusta Trevirorum (Trier in Germany) shows a panther pursuing a chariot and driver.

The *hoplomachus* is easily mistaken for the Thracian, as their equipment is all but the same. He could be distinguished by the rounded bronze shield and the long spear he used as a primary weapon. The representations of *hoplomachii* gladiators show the upper legs heavily padded with quilted defences, which compensated for the small size of the shield.

Looking from the amphitheatre gateway on to the arena floor at Pompeii. For many fighters this would have been their last moment to collect themselves before being assaulted by the colour, sunlight and applause that greeted them as they stepped outside. (Author's photograph)

The *provocator* was regarded as a middleweight gladiator. His shield was large and he was armed with a *gladius*, but over his chest he wore a *cardiophylax*, the half-breastplate secured by straps across his back. One victorious fighter wears a breastplate of this type on the Pompeii relief of AD 20–50. The *provocator* helmet, in the early empire, was rather like that of a *secutor*, but later appears to adopt a very different design, becoming bulbous, similar to that found on a Smyrna grave *stele*.

There remained another style of 'fighter' who started the combats between fighters at the *ludi* (schools). The *paegniarii* were used solely to whet the audience's appetite for what was to come. They were armed with wooden *rudis* swords and wore wrappings about their bodies to protect themselves from blows. They may have worn protective padding over their heads, but the Pompeii relief is damaged and indistinct. While the *paegniarii* fought they were accompanied by music played on cymbals, trumpets and the remarkable *hydraulis*, the water organ. The water organ appears on a number of sculptures and mosaics from the start of the empire, one of which is in the British Museum.

The *paegniarii* were very popular at the Colosseum games staged by the emperor Commodus. Dio Cassius reports that the emperor used the warm-up to display even more extravagant spectacle and costumes. He collected together all the lower body amputees in the city of Rome and, having fashioned serpents' tails about their stumps of legs and feet, beat them to death with a club as would some Herculean slayer of monsters.

Stage hands and arena equipment

The *paegniarii* were not supposed to fight to the death, and although high-ranking gladiators, the *primi pali*, died in the arena, it was usually the *tirones*, the trainees, who were killed. Their bodies were removed not with hooks, as is commonly believed, but were taken out on a cart. One mosaic in the archaeological museum in Tripoli shows what appears to be a casualty evacuation cart, which seems remarkably similar to a modern wheeled hospital bed. It was not only used to remove injured gladiators but also would have enabled the physicians to treat their wounds at a convenient height.

Behind every spectacle was a small army of workers. As a blast on a *tuba* (the straight trumpet) sounded, the gladiators would emerge from the dark tunnels, the *carceres*, of the amphitheatre. The scene shifters, the *libitinarii*, whose duty it was to remove the dead, were dressed as Hermes Psychopompus, the god who escorted the dead to the underworld. This was not their only task, however. Equipped with a hot iron rod, they would burn the flesh of a prone gladiator to check whether he was trying to fake his death. Hermes would then give way to another official, Charon, the ferryman of the dead. According to the Christian writer Tertullian, this representation of the mythological escort over the subterranean River Styx was dressed in black cloak, black boots and wore a mask representing the hook-nosed death demon of Etruscan legend. He would take a mallet and club the faking gladiator to death. There could be no escape from death if this was the audience's choice. A gladiator's throat was cut when he was removed to the *spoliarium* to be stripped of his armour. The bodies of criminals who died in the mass battles of the arena were dragged out and thrown into rivers or buried.

Weapons and shields

Danaos the Thracian, plumed and defended, would be ready to take up his trademark weapons. He was armed with the *sica*, a scimitar-like curved blade, sometimes shown with a shell-shaped guard in which he placed his hand. Variations of this shape are found on sculptures and mosaics, the blade shape being referred to as Danubian or Etruscan depending on the angle of curvature. A remarkable curved-bladed weapon made of iron is preserved in the Romermuseum, Augst, Switzerland and it is generally believed to be of gladiatorial origin.

This copy of a 2nd century relief carving shows a gladiator entrenched behind his shield. Armed with the small square *scutum*, this Thracian fighter uses it to the best advantage. (Author's photograph)

Both the *sica* and the *gladius* (the short straight sword) were tied on to the fighter's wrist to enable quick retrieval if they were dropped in combat. A marble relief in the National Museum of Rome shows a braided cord tied around the wrist of each fighter which is knotted around the sword pommel.

To defend himself against the incoming blows of his adversary the Thracian was defended with a square shield, the *parma* or *parmula*. These small wooden shields gave adequate defence to the upper body without being too heavy. The rounded bronze shields discovered at Pompeii have now been identified as belonging to the Thracian's close colleague, the *hoplomachus*. One example from the excavations bears a silver boss shaped as a Medusa head. It is 370mm (nearly 1¼ ft) in diameter and weighs 1.6kg (3½ lb) and was almost certainly made for decorative show. Combat versions of these bronze shields are commonly featured in mosaics and paintings. The British Museum in London has a very fine example of a bronze *hoplomachus* shield that has punched and incised patterning about its circumference.

The *myrmillo* was equipped with a larger shield than the Thracian, more in the style of the legionary *scutum*. Trajan's Column, the monument to the successes of the Dacian wars, does not show legionaries using the

largest imperial *scuta*. Those represented on the column and those in gladiatorial art are invariably smaller, although military shields found in archaeological excavations are sometimes larger. One large example found in Kasr el Harit in Egypt would have provided excellent protection in the arena, but as audiences wanted to see blood, gladiatorial shields seem to have been designed and issued with the express purpose of denying serious protection to the user. A large imperial *scutum* would be very difficult to penetrate although admittedly if it was used in the arena, it would encourage the use of skill to circumvent it. Its occasional use may have resulted in a static and dull encounter. This would account for the remarks of Julius Caesar, who found the games boring and would catch up on his reading when he tired of watching! Even Marcus Aurelius said he would not object to the games but for the fact they went on for so long.

Wooden shields were manufactured from a series of thin planked strips which, when laminated and glued, gave the strength to resist blows. Some of the shields found at archaeological sites in Europe and the Middle East have been covered with stitched linen and leather before their final paintwork has been applied over the surface. There is no reason to assume that gladiatorial shields would be any different in construction. Iron bosses, such as the examples recovered from military sites at Mainz in Germany, have been copied by modern armourers recreating gladiatorial equipment. One marble relief of two gladiators in the archaeological museum of Naples clearly shows the grip of the gladiatorial shield, which runs horizontally across the back of the boss, with a hole cut for the knuckles.

GLADIATOR PSYCHOLOGY

Gladiators were aware that death could strike them at any time. From the cells of the lowest ranks of gladiators at the Pompeii barracks, to the vastly superior billets of the greatest fighters, wall niches housed their gods. Hercules was very popular, together with Mars the god of war and Diana the huntress. A curse tablet found at the gladiatorial arena at Caerleon in Wales tells an interesting tale of attempted match fixing. The writer has stolen some clothing of another fighter and requires the intervention of Nemesis the goddess: 'Lady Nemesis, I give thee a cloak and a pair of boots. Let him who wears them not redeem them, except with his life's blood!'

But if life in the arena was short and brutal then life in the barracks was little better. The *lanista* and his *doctores* promoted aggression in the arena by imposing a tough regime in the barracks. Security guards were constantly vigilant for suicides. Tragic stories of gladiators who could not face their future are all too common. One Germanic gladiator choked himself to death by ramming the ancient sponge equivalent of toilet paper down his throat. Symmachus, a wealthy pagan politician eager to win votes by laying on a games, mentions the 29 Frankish prisoners he purchased, who strangled each other rather than fight in the arena. The last remaining fighter smashed his head against the wall until he died.

Despite their harsh life, strong esprit de corps emerged among gladiators. Even though he was the lowest of the low in society, a young

myrmillo gladiator bitterly complained when the the emperor Tiberius reduced the number of gladiatorial shows in an effort to reduce expenditure. The classical writer Seneca the Younger reported the fighter as saying 'his time was being wasted'. Other gladiators also preferred to fight rather than stagnate in the barracks. Even with this in mind, gladiators would observe the hierarchy that existed among them, and would rather fight a gladiator of equal rank than one of a lesser score.

To the gladiator, the attractions of combat outweighed the danger of their occupation. After a contest it became the practice for a plate to be passed about the stands for appreciative members of the audience to place their purses. A 3rd-century mosaic from Smirat in Tunisia shows a plate and four purses of money being presented to a fighter by an *editor* called Magerius. In an age where status was not only expressed by material wealth but also by whether one was free or enslaved, these cash prizes offered limited potential. There are extreme cases of gladiators of the highest orders being given generous gifts by their public. The *myrmillo* called Spiculus so impressed Nero that he made the fighter gifts of houses and properties equal to those owned by generals who had earned triumphs for their military conquests. Even though gladiatorial winnings were limited in AD 177 to 2,000 sesterces, a prize fund of 50,000 was offered after one fight at a later date than this.

To a freeman these splendid gifts spelled status and prosperity. To a serving gladiator, owned by a school, they were of crucial importance. Still locked into his five-year term of service, they were his ticket out of that life. Used as a bargaining lever, large prizes could buy a gladiator's path to freedom.

The *rudis*

For the vast majority of fighters there would only be one practical way out alive, however. Gladiators would fight in the arena hoping to win the *rudis*, the wooden sword of freedom, presented when they were deemed to have exhibited sufficient courage and skill. The slim chances of survival were set off by the life that could be achieved. Even if not actually free, gladiators could become famous in the eyes of their public, the *amatores*. This draw of fame, and their confidence in the arena, sent many gladiators back to their old ways even after the *rudis* had been presented. Flamma, a Syrian fighter, was offered the wooden sword four times, but signed on again and again. As a freeman he was offered the choice of continuing to fight, training his younger pupils as a *doctor*, or both. Flamma chose the latter and lived to the age of retirement, in his

The amphitheatre at Pompeii. As the dawn broke on the day of the games, the open area in the foreground would be filled with the audience browsing the stalls selling gladiatorial themed goods. Compare the accuracy of this modern photograph with the wall painting completed in AD 59 (see page 57). (Author's photograph)

case 30. His career brought him 25 victories, four *missus* (he was the loser but was spared), and nine *stans missus* (both fighters were declared the winner). Assuming he started fighting at the age of 17, that is an average of one potentially lethal fight every four months, although he may well have fought more in one month than another. His family inscribed his gravestone with records of his many wins.

Another gladiator named Bato won his match, but was surprised to see the immediate introduction of another opponent. He struggled to fight, but was again declared the winner. The emperor Caracalla, enjoyed this particular kind of tension, and introduced a third successive fighter, who not surprisingly overcame the now exhausted Bato and killed him. Bato was, however, honoured with a spectacular funeral.

Not all fighters were so popular. In death, gladiators were still despised. At Sassina, the new cemetery barred three classes of dead: those who had hung themselves, those of immoral trades … and gladiators.

The sheer resolve of the gladiators to actually step into the arena and face death impressed Dionysius of Halicarnassus. He was amazed at the steadfast courage the fighters exhibited as they watched their fellows struck down, saw the corpses carried away and the sand replenished to cover the bloodstains. What particularly impressed the public was the ability of gladiators to fight against a fellow fighter from the same school, knowing that his actions could result in the death of someone he was eating with in the mess hall only a few hours before. It would be

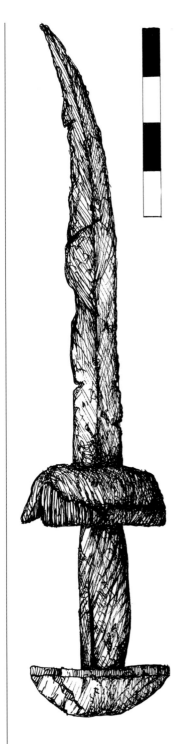

Wooden *rudis* training sword found at Oberaden in Germany. Though discovered in a ditch at a legionary site, this practice sword is identical to those used by gladiators in the barracks. The measurement bar indicates 10cm (3.94in). (Author's illustration)

somewhat more acceptable to a modern audience if a gladiator from one school killed an opponent from another, where his foe was a stranger, but that was not the case. Gladiators were taught to receive their death wounds and blows without uttering a sound. Sometimes, often paired by the drawing of lots, the *composito*, they faced a fellow pupil of their school. They may have trained with him, bathed with him and slept alongside him. Now they were expected to kill him.

Here the visored helmets, menacing and attractive in design, separated the man from the image. The sword killed not the mess mate from the dining hall, but the faceless *myrmillo* fish creature. The helmet (in all but the *retiarius*) was not removed as one gladiator killed another. The doomed gladiator merely knelt down to 'take the iron' (*ferrum recipere*) sometimes embracing the legs of his killer.

The public, eager to see the fighters before they stepped on to the sand of the arena, were curious to witness the behaviour of men who knew that death might be not far away. Before the day of the fights, the *editor* of the games would provide a lavish meal for the fighters, the *cena libera*. Those members of tomorrow's audience who were swept up in the whole drama of the games could view this spectacle, passing about the table watching the next morning's gladiators. As they did so they took voyeuristic pleasure from watching the guests abandon themselves to their possible fate. Some, the Thracians and Celts in particular, ate gluttonously. The Greeks took the opportunity to say goodbye to friends, and others, full of fear for the morning, were unable to eat, 'giving way to lamentation' as Plutarch stated. Others exercised moderation at the meal, eating wisely in the belief that they would increase their chances in the fighting of the next day.

If they were unfortunate enough to lose their fights, then the gladiator might not necessarily be executed. (The Hollywood image of thumbs down for death is probably a modern notion invented by film directors to register clearly on camera.) The winners (*victores*) would be presented with their palm branch of victory, the *palma*, or a crown of laurel wreaths, the *corona*, signifying a particularly outstanding win. An appreciative audience might spare the life of the loser. Many gladiators were recorded as being *missus*, a loser allowed to survive. Two gladiators who faced each other at the end of the fight, neither having fallen, were called *stantes* (the standing).

The sudden blow which unexpectedly despatched a fighter was less common than the disabling blow which reduced a fighter to his knees. As he held out his left hand index figure in a gesture of surrender, his fate lay in the hands of the audience. Reliefs and mosaics showing the moment of cold-blooded execution sometimes show the loser with his knees together in a position associated, in Roman eyes, with effeminacy. This was a slur continually being cast at the more attractive, handsome gladiators by jealous male spectators. The writer Juvenal suggests that the *retiarii* were the worst for soft effeminacy. Even their fellow gladiators regarded them as the lowest of the low within the school, partly because, whilst all the best gladiators could adopt stage names, the attractive young *retiarii* adopted the names of mythical figures of love like Narcissus and Cupid, well known for their beauty and romance. Their oiled muscular sex appeal was a huge draw for the young women of the audience, but to Juvenal one *retiarius* in particular, Gracchus by name, was beneath contempt.

'He fights, but not with the arms of a swordsman, Not with a dagger or shield (he hates and despises such weapons). What he hurls is a net, and he misses of course, and we see him look up at the seats, then run for his life, all around the arena. Easy for all to know and identify. Look at his tunic golden cord and fringe, and that queer, conspicuous arm guard!'

Gladiators who fell in combat, being outside respectable society, would not be permitted an honourable burial, unless there were family, friends or admirers who would claim his body. The *lanista* of the troop occasionally financed the graves of the fallen, but almost always for the reasons of publicity. Often it was only the comrades of the dead gladiator who had lived and fought with him who saw he was remembered after his death.

THE GLADIATOR IN COMBAT

'*Ave Caesar, morituri te salutant!*'
('We who are about to die salute the Emperor.')

Though Hollywood would have us believe every gladiatorial combat began in this fashion, not every match resulted in the actual death of a fighter. The gladiators of the highest grades, having had such vast sums expended on their training and preparation, were unlikely to be 'wasted' on a whim of the crowd. We do know that veterans suffered at the hands of keen trainees. The Pompeiian graffiti showing the combat between the old hand Hilarus, a *Thraex,* and the newly trained *myrmillon,* Attilius, reveals that the victor was not the veteran, but the young *tiro.* The audience spared Hilarus, and Attilius fought Raecius Felix, armed as a *Thraex,* conquering him also.

When the *noxii,* the criminals, made the salute to their emperor they did so because they genuinely knew that their death was fast approaching. As disposable performers in the massed battle re-enactments they knew they would be killed. The judicial system practised punishment and execution in the arenas, and the governing bodies emptied the prisons to provide fighters. They became part of the mass spectacle of classical warfare, often naval warfare, presented for the enjoyment of the public on manmade lakes. Famous naval victories could now be re-enacted for the mob.

The naval engagements recreated for the public were called the *naumachiae.* They were originated by Julius Caesar, who dug a special lake at the Field of Mars near Rome. When filled with water, this artificial lake could hold 16 full-size war galleys manned by 4,000 oarsmen. Aboard the boats 2,000 prisoners, armed as Rome's enemies, were ordered to fight to the death. The emperor Titus, hearing how popular the fights had been with the people, had a permanent lake constructed and emptied the prisons, using dispensable prisoners for the displays. His recreation of the marine battle of Salamis exceeded anything seen at arena-based games. There was savage fighting by the pressed criminals and prisoners of war, who had virtually no chance of a reprieve. There was a very slim chance that those who

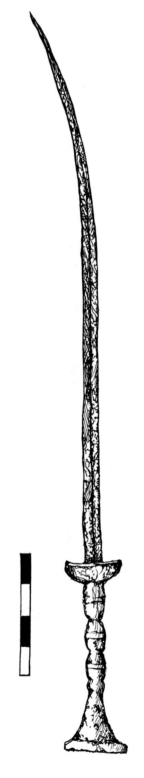

Iron-bladed weapon which is interpreted as a variant on the Thracian *sica* sword. The measurement bar indicates 10cm (3.94in). (Author's illustration)

Relief tombstone of the retired gladiator Danaos. By the time of his death Danaos had married Heorte, and had a son Asklepliades. We do not know whether Danaos was a gladiatorial volunteer, and thus free to marry any time he wished, or whether he won the right of release and the freedom to wed. (Author's illustration)

showed extraordinary courage might be spared.

The now famous gladiatorial salute was first recorded during the reign of the emperor Claudius. Suetonius records the doomed crews of vessels drawing up to the imperial podium and shouting 'Hail Emperor, greetings from the men about to die', whereupon the emperor stupidly shouted back 'or perhaps not!' The crews took this to mean that they might not die at all, and presumed they had received an Imperial pardon, so they began to move their vessels apart. The audience went into near riot, Claudius flew into a rage and threatened to send in troops to massacre them. The presence of *balistae* and other artillery was not uncommon at the *naumachiae*. Claudius often positioned thousands of troops on rafts to suppress any uprising or break-out by the performers. Backing away from the military option of sinking the day's entertainment and drowning the performers, Claudius walked to the water's edge, where he managed to coax the performers into combat.

The arena-based combats, vast though they sometimes were, never saw the mass casualties of the *naumachia* or, indeed, the huge audiences. It is reported that 500,000 people watched the *naumachia* on the Fucine Lake 96.5km (60 miles) east of Rome. Compared with this, audiences for the arena games were small, though they followed the events in the arena very seriously and it is a testimony to the power of the spectacle that it could provoke such emotion. In AD 59 a riot broke out in the Pompeii amphitheatre. Tacitus reported that 'about this time there was a serious fight between the inhabitants of Nuceria and Pompeii. It arose out of a trifling incident at a gladiatorial show. Abuse led to stone throwing, and swords were drawn. The people of Pompeii, where the show was being held, came off best. Many wounded and mutilated were taken to the capital. The Emperor instructed the Senate to investigate the affair. When they reported back the Senate debarred Pompeii from holding any similar gathering for ten years. The sponsor of the show and his fellow instigators of the disorder were exiled.'

The build-up

A typical games was advertised by notices painted in red ochre on a whitewashed wall, no doubt with a hundred similar notices obscured beneath. One survives on a whitewashed wall in Rome: 'Weather permitting, 30 pairs of gladiators, furnished by A. Clodius Flaccus, together with substitutes in case any get killed too quickly, will fight 1st, 2nd, 3rd of May. The fights will be followed by a wild beast hunt. The famous gladiator Paris will fight. Hurrah for Paris! Hurrah for the generous Flaccus, who is running for duumvirate!' Beneath the advertising organised by Flaccus the aspiring politician, the signwriter had also painted 'Marcus wrote this by the light of the moon…' This sight was repeated all over the empire. The whitewashed, graffiti-covered walls of Pompeii still bear an advertisement for games held by one Lucretius Satrius.

The throngs of modern tourists in the narrow streets of Pompeii must resemble the crowds of Romans heading to the amphitheatre at the town's Porta di Sarno gate. The *loca*, or capacity of Pompeii's amphitheatre was 20,000, a large number for a comparatively small town. We can assume that people came from outside the town, as notices are found on masonry and stones some distance outside the busy commercial centres of the town itself. As they walked to the open piazza in front of the impressive main entrance (still exactly as it was found, and in remarkable condition) they were encouraged to buy souvenirs from market stalls, such as lamps, glassware and pottery all fashioned with a gladiatorial theme. At Pompeii the dark *vomitoria*, the entry tunnel to the smaller tunnels beneath the seating, is now blackened by centuries of dust and grime, but it is still possible to see traces of the original wall colouring of yellow ochre and black. At the Colosseum, bone or clay tickets called *tesserae* were issued to help spectators find their seats. They would have been distributed free in the weeks before the fights, on the wishes of the *editor* of the games, and ticket holders would be led to their seat by ushers called *locarii* ('they who give a location').

The *maeniana* and the *cavea*, the stands, were arranged in rank order with the positions nearest to the action being sought after by members of higher social classes. Those persons who had not been issued tickets stood with the non-citizens, the *peregrini*, because of their poor social class. At the highest tier of the Colosseum stood the *pullati*, the very poor. Rather like some modern sporting events today, it was important

Graffiti of two gladiators of unknown style facing each other in combat, from the theatre complex wall in Pompeii (see page 53 for the original images *in situ*). (Author's illustration)

to be seen in the best part of the stands, to emphasise one's social standing. Juvenal writes of the bastard sons of gladiators seeking to better themselves in the public eye, pressuring some of the elevated classes, to make them leave their superior seats in the arena stands: '"Out of the front row seats!" they cry when you're out of money. "Yield your place to the sons of some pimp, the spawn of some cat-house, some slick auctioneer's brat, or the louts some trainer has fathered, or the well-groomed boys whose sire is a gladiator."'

The *carcere* tunnels, leading to the seating, were host to every kind of marketer, from prostitutes to food sellers. Members of the audience who grew bored with the activities of the arena could make their way below. As the show developed, the excitement of the audience grew in volume. Classical writers describe the sound of the people like 'surf in a storm'. Working through the audience would be sellers of food and people bearing banners, *tabellae*, with up-to-date lists of the fighters. As soon as the final *Libellius Munerarius*, the programme lists of paired fighters were available betting would be rife. Ovid suggests that borrowing a programme from a likely female was a good way of meeting girls, though the seating order in amphitheatres was segregated between the sexes on the orders of Augustus. The front rows were reserved for senators, with soldiery, married men and pupils and teachers also sitting apart. The women sat in the uppermost rows at the back.

Above the spectators billowed an awning, the *vela*, supported by masts held atop the perimeter wall of the amphitheatre. We can assume that most amphitheatres had an awning of this kind. One is clearly shown on the Pompeii wall painting of the amphitheatre. Archaeologists have long argued about the practical physics of how this awning was supported and only recently have settled on a levered boom approach, operated by block and tackle from above. Contemporary accounts report that it was made of wool, canvas being too heavy. It also appears on the Colosseum, at least, to be dyed red ochre, as we are told, the light shining through it created waves of constantly changing coloured light over the sand.

The effectiveness of the awning can be clearly demonstrated by one notorious emperor's now infamous orders in the Colosseum. On a scorching hot day the audience seemed ungrateful for a show staged by the emperor. He ordered the sailors responsible for rigging the awning to furl the fabric and, unable to escape the sun's glare and escape through the now deliberately locked doors, members of the audience began to collapse with sunstroke. To keep the arena cool on other occasions, scented water fountains, the *sparsiones*, operated.

The arena sand itself was specially imported. Nero is reputed to have ordered gold dust sprinkled on the surface to catch the light, but this may be a misinterpretation of the fact that Caligula and Nero favoured coloured dusts, in greenish blue and red oxide of lead vermilion, instead of normal sand.

The bowl shape of amphitheatres reflects heat inwards and the sound outwards. Every sound made by the gladiators would have been clearly audible, even to those in the highest seats, hence the ruling that gladiators should withstand their injuries in silence. Even at the highest, poorest status seating, the audience could see the battle clearly. The architecture afforded everyone in the audience a clear view of the

action, allowing the character Echion, in Petronius Arbiter's, 1st-century play *Satyricon*, to satisfy his desire to see 'cold steel, no quarter and a slaughterhouse right in the middle where all the stands can see it!'

With the audience assembled, the games could begin. The task of introducing the proceedings fell to the *praecones* (narrators) whose job it would be to announce the day's presentation. The holders of the games were allowed to wear the robes and dress of high officials. Petronius uses his character Echion to hold forth on such matters. Speaking of a potential politician putting up the finance for a games he says '... and he's got the wherewithal – he was left 30 million when his poor father died. Even if he spent four hundred thousand, his pocket won't feel it and he'll go down in history. He's got some big brutes already and a woman who fights in a chariot ... If he really does it he'll make off with all Norbanus' votes, I'll tell you he'll win at a canter!'

The performers, the famous *venatores* and the gladiators, would have arrived by cart and chariot. Depending on the money he was willing to pay out for his exhibition of self-aggrandisement, the *editor* of the games could plan an extravagant entrance. It was not unknown for nobles and emperors to arrive drawn by the black and white tiger horse, the African zebra.

The parade in the arena: early morning

It was very important that the *editor* showed his face as much as possible during the *pompa*, the parade in the arena. The relief carving from

Pompeii shows slaves carrying the gladiators' armour. Trumpet players, *tibicenes*, provided the music and slaves carried a *ferculum* on their shoulders, a platform which displayed martial statuary of the war gods: Mars, Hercules, Nemesis and Victory. While the other gladiators were issued with their helmets in the *carcere* tunnels, the audience began to tire of the *pompa*, an obvious political ploy. The expression 'as tiresome as a circensian procession' became common.

The *venatio*: beast hunting

The morning would begin with the *venatio*, a beast hunt. The barriers, that spanned the 'gates of life', the *Porta Sanavivaria*, and that of death, the *Porta Libitinesis*, would be opened and the unfortunate animals released into the arena. The creatures killed in the *venatio* had been captured all over Europe and the known parts of Africa and the Middle East. With the *venatio* over, the dead creatures were dragged from the arena. The sun would be higher, mid-way through the morning, and the smell of blood and offal rising in the heat beneath the awning. Music and singing would draw the attention of the audience away from the activity in the arena below. Some nobles returned home for dinner. Seneca believed that the savagery of the next show was only suitable for the mob.

The theatre tunnel where the spectators of Pompeii stood while waiting to be seated in the auditorium beyond the wall. The walls here have a fascinating collection of period graffiti, including Roman warships, gladiators and fighting horses. (Author's photograph)

The afternoon show: the *noxii*

Excavations at Pompeii have not yet revealed a prison, but at least an eighth of the site still lies beneath a blanket of ash, so it may emerge. Assuming this provincial town had its share of criminal classes, the games probably followed the same pattern as elsewhere. After the *venatio*, the *noxii* provided the entertainment. The criminals, dispossessed and prisoners of war who were paraded into the arena were sometimes given weapons and armour and told to fight until just one of them remained. Seneca wrote 'What is the need for defensive armour or for skill? All these mean delaying death. In the morning they throw men to the lions and the bears, at noon they throw them to the spectators. The spectators demand that the slayer shall face the man who is to slay him in his turn, and they keep the latest victor for another butchering … That sort of thing goes on until the arena is empty.'

Occasionally, unarmoured men were 'exhibition killed' by highly efficient, veteran gladiators, perhaps the *postulati*, in full armour with ball and mace. Even if one armed a member of the *noxii*, the audience would not know whether he was actually an official gladiator, but it gave the impression that he had received training and had a fighting chance.

Inevitably, he would be felled by the veteran. It was simply a way of turning official executions into display.

The *familia gladiatoria*

The nobility returned to their seats for the highlight of the games, when the gladiatorial schools showed their skills; every gladiator from the lowest ranking *meridiani*, the second-class school fighters, to the *primi pali*, fighters of the highest grades, competed for their reputations and prize money. The fighters made their way into the arena to the sound of trumpet blasts and music from the water organs about the arena wall. They probably made some salute to the *editor* of the games.

The *meridiani* fighters fought in pairs, drawn by lots. Their weapons were tested in the *probatio armorum* ceremony, which aimed to prove to the public that the weapons were sharp. The trumpets sounded and the gladiators, more than just two fighting pairs, spread their combats about the circumference of the arena. They would not fight alone, however. Their trainers, the *doctores* from the schools, would give them commands, suggestions and advice on the weak spots of the enemy. In addition, slaves stood ready to whip and beat the fighters with leather whips or *lora*, if the *doctores* felt their performance was lacking style or will.

As gladiators were badly injured, the trumpet would sound and spectators leapt up to cry '*Habet! hoc Habet!*' or 'Got him! He's had it!' Now came the moment of appeal. The *editor* watched closely as the fallen fighter raised his hand. His fate, whether released, *missus*, still to live, or *periit*, to be killed, now lay in the hands of the audience. Historians have argued for many years about the hand action for death, made by the audience. The current view is that fist and thumb jabbing upward accompanied by a cry of '*Iugula*' meant kill him; and the thumb down meant weapons to the ground, and let him live. Assuming that the unfortunate *meridiani* fighters, all of whom were poor quality *tirones*, were dispensable, then death would usually be inflicted by stabbing or slashing the back of the neck, or with a cut across the throat with a sword or dagger. This would be a relatively speedy death, probably caused by the severing of the spinal cord. Some mosaics and wall paintings show the gladiator kneeling, embracing the legs of the victor as the *gladius* is positioned to

Bignor Villa in West Sussex, UK, houses a remarkable Roman mosaic showing cherubs locked in battle and dressed in gladiatorial armour. In addition to the *retiarii* and *secutor* shown here is a *doctor* (fight trainer) together with his beating stick for encouraging lazy fighters. (With thanks to the Tupper family, Bignor Roman Villa, West Sussex, England)

This relief carving shows *pontarii* fighters on a bridge. The bridge could be used to hold any combination of gladiators. (Author's illustration)

sever the spinal cord. The dead man's body was removed by trolley and slaves stripped the armour from him. Slaves un-officially sold gladiators' blood to epileptics, who believed it had the power to cure them.

After the second-rate trainees had performed their shows, the famous fighters would be brought on. Our man Danaos would feature in this part of the day. It would now be mid-to late afternoon, usually the signal for the sailors aloft to furl the *vela* awning. This was sometimes difficult, particularly with the huge expanse of cloth over an amphitheatre as large as the Colosseum. The upward rush of the escaping warm air made the fabric very difficult to handle.

One of the afternoon's combats was to be between Negrimus, a *retiarius,* and Priedens, his *secutor* opponent. Whether these fighters were, in reality, top-class fighters or mere *meridiani* is lost to us but their action is described on a wall at Pompeii. Danaos would fight his opponent after them. After the trumpet call, the fighters circled each other, seeking the opportunity to catch their opposite off guard. The *secutor* was looking to hide behind his large *scutum* and close on the *retiarius,* but the *retiarius* used his mobility to keep at a distance and strike with his trident, quickly dropping the prongs into the sand to prevent it snagging on his own net. The *rete,* as it was called, was thrown but did not fully disable the *secutor,* who rushed forward still beneath the enveloping web. Struck in the leg, Negrimus fell, but recovered himself as the *secutor* came forward again, stabbing Negrimus who was hit in his net arm. Though the *secutor* was held off by the trident, he was protected with his rectangular shield and still carried a *gladius.* For reasons unknown to us, Negrimus, though again struck in the leg, suddenly managed to get the advantage on the *secutor,* Priedens, and struck at his feet with his long trident, crippling the *secutor,* who made the sign for mercy. After a moment, reflecting the mood of the audience, the *editor* gave his decision. The *secutor* Priedens was to die. Negrimus, wounded in both legs and in his net arm, had not the energy to despatch the *secutor* so he motioned to another *retiarius* named Hippolytus to help him. Meanwhile, Priedens knelt to accept the death blow without a sound. Hippolytus' sword was placed at the throat of the still helmeted Priedens. Negrimus simply pushed his victim on to the blade from behind. The act was over. The *retiarius* earned the winnings of the victor, the fame and public attention, and a palm branch. His name was recorded with the V of the victor in the scoresheets. For Priedens there would be only the symbol ϴ, the Greek letter for TH, the word *thanatos*, meaning 'death'.

Even though Danaos' tombstone stands in the Kunsthistoriches Museum in Vienna, Austria, we know very little of his life. It would not be correct to insert his name over another, better recorded, combat of a Thracian fighter purely to complete this part of the narrative. How Danaos gained his freedom, be it buying his way out through winnings, or being voted the *rudis* by an *editor*, we will never know. If he had been awarded the *rudis* by the audience, his *lanista* would be given the fighter's market value by the *editor* of the games. Similarly, if Danaos was severely injured during a *munus*, and released from service by his *lanista*, then again the *editor* would pay. We do not know the events of Danaos' last fight, but let us assume on the ninth fight of his gladiatorial career he has been declared *victor*, the winner.

Mounting a set of steps (at Pompeii there were probably wooden steps temporarily erected from the arena floor) to the *editor's* podium, he was awarded the palm branch of victory. As graffiti from Pompeii shows, he would have returned to the arena floor, lapping the circumference, proudly waving the symbol of victory above his head. He is still in his helmet. If a gladiator's performance had been particularly worthy, the *editor* of the games presented him with the *rudis*, the wooden sword that symbolised freedom. Whether a *rudis* was actually given to each freed gladiator to keep, or was merely a public symbol on the day is unclear, but as it meant that the gladiator never had to wield a sword in anger again, the author believes it was presented as a gift.

A dead fighter, if sufficiently famous and popular, would be treated to a lavish funerary procession. Most of the un-fortunates who fell would be lucky if they received a funeral paid for by their fellow fighters, a lover from a grand house, or their sponsor. If Priedens was *primus palus*, the highest grade, he would have a grand procession, his bier bedecked perhaps in amber as Nero honoured his fallen fighters. The public who loved him in life would be there to mourn him in death. Spontaneous acts of mourning often occurred at

The amphitheatre of AD 59 during the riots that caused Pompeii to be barred from holding games for a period of ten years.
Note the *vellarium* awning is erected in this scene. On the original wall painting, now in Naples City Museum, advertising slogans for games can be seen on the buildings nearby.
(Author's illustration)

the funerals of famous gladiators. One young man, unable to live without his beloved gladiator hero, is said to have thrown himself on to the funeral pyre and was himself consumed.

Danaos was now a free man, possessing also the *praemium*, or purse collection from some of the 20,000 people in the audience. He had several options open to him. Like the Syrian fighter Flamma, he could return to the schools as a freeman, and continue his career as a fighter, or he could try to be accepted as a *doctor* of a school, and teach the Thracian way of fighting to new trainees. Flamma actually chose to return to fighting, but Danaos decided he would retire. Free gladiators could even become *lanistae* themselves, using their winnings to finance the purchase of new *tirones* from the slave markets.

RETIREMENT

The image of the retired gladiator drinking at an inn and telling tales of his experiences is a cosy one, and perhaps not without some truth. No evidence survives, but there are a few records of them marrying and settling down. Gladiators inspired feelings of desire in both sexes. The expensive jewellery found on the female body in the barrack room at Pompeii may be the remains of the last liaison between a wealthy lady and her gladiator lovers. The word is used in plural as there were eight other men in the room with her when she died. Juvenal delivers a damning condemnation of a woman called Eppia, who by eloping with an ageing ex-gladiator has ruined her name. He questions …

> 'What was the youthful charm that Eppia found so enchanting? What did she see worthwhile in being labelled 'the Gladiatress?' This dear boy had begun to shave a long while ago, and one arm, wounded, gave hope of retirement. Besides he was frightfully ugly, scarred by his helmet, a wart on his nose, and his eyes always running. Gladiators always look better than any Adonis: That is what she preferred to children, country, and sister. This, to her husband … The sword is what they dote on, these women!'

Danaos' family erected his tombstone in the 2nd century AD. He had married his wife Heorte, and had a son called Asklepiades. His family dog seems to be shown on the tombstone, but the creature is the symbol for death and may be misleading.

Chances of survival

The chances of gladiators surviving to retire were, by the nature of their job, even worse than legionaries if some modern calculations are to be believed. *Munera*, which were primarily staged to demonstrate superiority between political rivals, had to outdo each other; the best shows were the bloodiest. During the republican period, it was announced in advance that fights would be *sine missus*, that is to say that the loser would definitely perish. Augustus put a stop to that practice and in the 1st century AD there seems to be a fair chance that losing fighters would be spared if they had showed enough courage. As the imperial age continued, however, harsh judicial and military regimes

imposed their will on the arena and gladiators again seem to suffer death more often than not. The historian Georges Ville studied 100 1st-century duels and found that only 19 out of the studied 200 gladiators died. That is a 9:1 chance of survival. By the 3rd century Ville calculated that the likelihood was that in every other fight, one of the combatants would die.

If Danaos survived to his 30th year, as did the Syrian Flamma, then he was above the average life expectancy of his fellows. Most tombstones of the 1st century AD show an average age of death of 27, but the vast majority of fighters would have perished between the ages of 18 to 25, as nerves and inexperience in front of thousands of wild-eyed people overcame them just at the point they needed their concentration the most. There are no tombstones for the unknown thousands of *tirones*, for whom there was no victory.

Graffiti from Pompeii depicting the combat between trainee fighter M[arcus] Attilius the *myrmillo* and the Thracian, Lucius Raecius Felix. The Thracian had a string of victories to his name when he faced the newcomer, but was soundly beaten by the *tiro* in only his second fight. He lived to fight again, however. (Author's illustration)

RE-ENACTMENT

For many years Roman army re-enactment has been popular. However, one group of British re-enactors form the Portsmouth-based Second Legion Augusta, and have assembled a troupe calling themselves the 'Gladiators of Vespasian'.

Following the success of the film *Gladiator*, a number of other British groups quickly put into practice what many had spoken about for several years. Within a year of the film's release, a number of re-enactment

familia gladiatoria and a highly professional corporate entertainment team had developed very entertaining and authentic shows. Dr Marcus Junklemann's team of gladiatorial reconstruction performers in Germany must rank as the most spectacular and remarkable creations that experimental archaeology has produced. The attention to detail is second to none. The Second Legion Augusta can be contacted at *legiiavg@cwcom.net*. A professional entertainment group has also developed a series of informative and exciting combat shows based around a gladiatorial theme, called Stunt-Action-Specialists. Contact: *mark@stuntaction.plus.com*

The expense of the equipment is not so great a problem as the difficulty in actually faking combat for an audience. Re-enactment sword fights of other periods, where doublets and jerkins can hide the lack of an obvious wound, pose fewer difficulties than near naked gladiators performing before an audience. With safety in mind, teams of modern performers have successfully represented gladiatorial combat, in locations such as the Museum of London and the British Museum.

'The familia gladiatoria erected this to Satornilos, to remember him' read the words on this tombstone to a Thracian fighter. Note the padded leggings that he wears beneath his greaves, and the palm branch identifying him as a victor. (Author's illustration)

BIBLIOGRAPHY

Grant, Michael, *Gladiators*, Penguin, 2000

Junkelmann, Dr Marcus *Das Spiel mit dem Todt – Roms Gladitoren im Experiment*, Philip Von Zabern, 2000

Kohne, Eckhart, and Ewigleben, Cornelia (Eds.), *The Power of Spectacle in Ancient Rome*, University of California Press, 2000

Juvenal, *Sixteen Satires*, Penguin, 1998

Byock, Jesse (Ed.), *Martial in English*, Penguin, 1996

Ovid, *The Erotic Poems*, Penguin, 1996

Petronius, *The Satyricon*, Penguin, 1997

Pliny, *The Letters of the Younger Pliny*, Penguin, 1997

Wiedemann, Thomas *Emperors and Gladiators*, Routledge, 1995

Auguet, Roland, *Cruelty and Civilization: The Roman Games*, Routledge, 1994

GLOSSARY

Amphitheatre purpose-built performing area for combats, having an elliptical arena

Arena the sand-filled fighting floor of an amphitheatre

Balteus sword belt

Carcere tunnels serving the centre of an amphitheatre

Cavea the seating inside an amphitheatre

Colosseum situated in Rome, the largest amphitheatre in the empire

Doctor fight-trainer in gladiatorial school

Editor individual sponsor of gladiatorial games

Fasciae quilted and padded leg defences

Fascina trident used by *retiarii*

Galea helmet

Galerus shoulder defence worn by *retiarii*

Gladius straight-bladed sword

Hoplomachus heavily armoured gladiator who fought with a round shield and spear

Lanista private entrepreneur who assembles teams of gladiators

Ludi schools, including those of gladiators; also, games

Manica arm defence, originally made from linen or leather but sometimes in metal

Meridiani second-class fighters

Missio reprieve from death in the arena

Munus (pl. *munera*) memorial games to honour the dead

Myrmillo gladiator armed as a legionary with large *scutum* and *gladius*

Naumachia sea battle

Noxii condemned criminals forced to fight to the death

Palus post for training sword blows against

Parmula round shield

Periit 'he has died'

Pompa procession preceding games

Praeco narrator in the arena

Primus Palus highest ranking gladiator

Provocator gladiator armed with *gladius* and *scutum*

Retiarius trident- and dagger-armed gladiator throwing the *rete*

Rete net used by *retiarii* gladiators

Rudis wooden training sword symbolic of gladiator's discharge

Secutor gladiator who wore close-fitting helmet

Scutum wooden shield, little different from legionary version

Sica curved sword

Subligaculum loincloth worn by gladiators

Thracian gladiator armed with curved *Sica* and small wooden shield

Tiro trainee

Venatio wild animal hunt preceding gladiatorial show

Venatores beast hunters in the arena

Velarium awning above an amphitheatre

THE COLOUR PLATES

A: RECRUITMENT

Slaves and new recruits are dragged into the barracks of an imperial school under the watchful eye of their new owner, the *lanista* of this troupe. Legionaries are posted at every doorway and corridor, where specially built guard points would give them the advantage in quelling an uprising among the inmates. A free gladiator, perhaps one who has returned to the trade after winning his release, watches the new arrivals, remembering the similar treatment of his arrival. They will be placed in the roughest cells of the barracks, not the relative comfort afforded to the veteran fighters.

B: TRAINING, POMPEII, AD 78

In the central arena of the school two new trainees practice with the *rudis*, the wooden sword, while a *doctor* (trainer) looks on. They are not trusted with sharp weapons, as the authorities feared a mutiny in the schools. The trainer holds a stick to encourage reticent fighters into action if their nerves are lacking. The barefoot gladiators are armed as a Thracian and a *secutor,* although the latter has removed his

A copy of a terracotta *hydraulis* (water organ) organist. A remarkable musical instrument, it was not loud, but played accompanying music during or between gladiatorial fights. The original, in the British Museum, London, shows an organist (now minus his head) playing the small portable machine. Doors in the arena wall gave access for musicians when the main doors were shut. (Author's photograph)

The Saffron Walden *retiarius*. This relief, originally from Caerleon in South Wales, has been ignored as a useful source of information, but close inspection reveals a square plate on the elbow of the *manica*. Modern reconstructions show that an elbow plate would give much better movement to a fighter using metal plate defences. (Saffron Walden Museum, Essex, England)

helmet to breathe more freely. The Thracian helmet afforded clearer vision and ventilation, and the likelihood is that this *secutor* is feeling the disadvantage of his armour. A *retiarius* practises on the far right, casting his net over the 2m (6¹/₂ft) high *palus*. All of the activity is watched by a richly dressed woman, who is visiting the schools in an effort to see her lover, a veteran fighter.

C: THE *RETIARIUS*

The *retiarius* is armed with his *rete* (1), the 3m (9³/₄ft) diameter net edged with lead weights (2), which could be used to whip the opposing fighter, to trip him or ensnare him, as shown in the sketch detail (3). The long cord (4) enabled him to tie it to his wrist, for immediate recovery after an unsuccessful cast. The trident (5) was the principal weapon of the *retiarius* and could be effective if thrust with both hands, should the net be lost. The tips of the trident could pose serious problems if caught on the net, and *retiarii* seem to have dug the prongs into the sand at the moment of throwing to avoid this problem. The *pugio* dagger (shown tucked into his waistband) could be used to cut the net cord

free if the *retiarius* found his opponent ensnared but not disabled, a position of danger. The *galerus* (6), or shoulder guard, provided enough protection for the *retiarius* to turn their bodies to face their foe with confidence: the inset example shows a particularly nautical theme on the relief. It was strapped around the upper arm (7). The *retiarius* also wears arm padding (8) to protect his lower arm from slashing and stabbing. He also wears a medallion charm (9), and a headband (10).

D: THRACIAN AND *SECUTOR*

The Thracian gladiator (A) is equipped with a smaller cut-down version of the traditional legionnary *scutum* shield (1). The universal canvas *manica* arm defence afforded adequate protection, but later periods saw the introduction of metal, scale and mail armour (2): an inside view of the construction is also shown (2a). The metal arm defences were held in place by leather strapping across the shoulders and chest, secured by a buckle (2b). The Thracian's helmet crest is topped with a griffin (3); the helmets found at Pompeii have fixings for extravagant plumes, as shown here. A detail is also shown of the eyepiece of this type of helmet (3a). The main difference in the armament of these fighters is the sword. The *secutor* (B) is equipped with a straight stabbing *gladius* (4), while the Thracian has a curved *sica* (5). The *secutor*, normally the traditional opponent of the *retiarius,* carries a large *scutum* (6), but has a plain helmet (7) to avoid potentially fatal snagging of the net, shown here in 'exploded view'. A *secutor* helmet found at Pompeii had both sides of the crest painted with red oxide. The *secutor*